C-1984   CAREER EXAMINATION SERIES

This is your
PASSBOOK for...

School Clerk

Test Preparation Study Guide
Questions & Answers

COPYRIGHT NOTICE

This book is SOLELY intended for, is sold ONLY to, and its use is RESTRICTED to individual, bona fide applicants or candidates who qualify by virtue of having seriously filed applications for appropriate license, certificate, professional and/or promotional advancement, higher school matriculation, scholarship, or other legitimate requirements of education and/or governmental authorities.

This book is NOT intended for use, class instruction, tutoring, training, duplication, copying, reprinting, excerption, or adaptation, etc., by:

1) Other publishers
2) Proprietors and/or Instructors of "Coaching" and/or Preparatory Courses
3) Personnel and/or Training Divisions of commercial, industrial, and governmental organizations
4) Schools, colleges, or universities and/or their departments and staffs, including teachers and other personnel
5) Testing Agencies or Bureaus
6) Study groups which seek by the purchase of a single volume to copy and/or duplicate and/or adapt this material for use by the group as a whole without having purchased individual volumes for each of the members of the group
7) Et al.

Such persons would be in violation of appropriate Federal and State statutes.

PROVISION OF LICENSING AGREEMENTS – Recognized educational, commercial, industrial, and governmental institutions and organizations, and others legitimately engaged in educational pursuits, including training, testing, and measurement activities, may address request for a licensing agreement to the copyright owners, who will determine whether, and under what conditions, including fees and charges, the materials in this book may be used them. In other words, a licensing facility exists for the legitimate use of the material in this book on other than an individual basis. However, it is asseverated and affirmed here that the material in this book CANNOT be used without the receipt of the express permission of such a licensing agreement from the Publishers. Inquiries re licensing should be addressed to the company, attention rights and permissions department.

All rights reserved, including the right of reproduction in whole or in part, in any form or by any means, electronic or mechanical, including photocopying, recording, or by any information storage and retrieval system, without permission in writing from the Publisher.

Copyright © 2025 by
National Learning Corporation

212 Michael Drive, Syosset, NY 11791
(516) 921-8888 • www.passbooks.com
E-mail: info@passbooks.com

PASSBOOK® SERIES

THE *PASSBOOK® SERIES* has been created to prepare applicants and candidates for the ultimate academic battlefield – the examination room.

At some time in our lives, each and every one of us may be required to take an examination – for validation, matriculation, admission, qualification, registration, certification, or licensure.

Based on the assumption that every applicant or candidate has met the basic formal educational standards, has taken the required number of courses, and read the necessary texts, the *PASSBOOK® SERIES* furnishes the one special preparation which may assure passing with confidence, instead of failing with insecurity. Examination questions – together with answers – are furnished as the basic vehicle for study so that the mysteries of the examination and its compounding difficulties may be eliminated or diminished by a sure method.

This book is meant to help you pass your examination provided that you qualify and are serious in your objective.

The entire field is reviewed through the huge store of content information which is succinctly presented through a provocative and challenging approach – the question-and-answer method.

A climate of success is established by furnishing the correct answers at the end of each test.

You soon learn to recognize types of questions, forms of questions, and patterns of questioning. You may even begin to anticipate expected outcomes.

You perceive that many questions are repeated or adapted so that you can gain acute insights, which may enable you to score many sure points.

You learn how to confront new questions, or types of questions, and to attack them confidently and work out the correct answers.

You note objectives and emphases, and recognize pitfalls and dangers, so that you may make positive educational adjustments.

Moreover, you are kept fully informed in relation to new concepts, methods, practices, and directions in the field.

You discover that you are actually taking the examination all the time: you are preparing for the examination by "taking" an examination, not by reading extraneous and/or supererogatory textbooks.

In short, this PASSBOOK®, used directedly, should be an important factor in helping you to pass your test.

SCHOOL CLERK

DUTIES
Prepares, maintains and inputs permanent record cards of pupils; prepares and issues transcripts of pupils' records to high schools, colleges and universities; requisitions materials and supplies as approved and checks upon delivery and issues to faculty members/staff. May be required to receive, count and deposit all monies that pass through the office and issues receipts and maintains financial records/reports of same. May operate telephone switchboard and other office equipment including typewriter, CRT terminal, personal computer, word processor, printer and related office equipment. May be required to open the school doors for callers to enter the building. May be required to take charge of the administrative office during summer months, when school is not in session or when directed by the Principal/Assistant Principal. Performs related duties as required.

SUBJECT OF EXAMINATION
The written test is designed to test for knowledge, skills, and/or abilities in such areas as:

1. **Office management** - These questions test for knowledge of the principles and practices of planning, organizing and controlling the activities of an office and directing those performing office activities so as to achieve predetermined objectives such as accomplishing office work within reasonable limits of time, effort and cost expenditure. Typical activities may include but will not be restricted to: simplifying and improving procedures, increasing office efficiency, improving the office work environment and controlling office supplies.
2. **Office record keeping** - These questions test your ability to perform common office record keeping tasks. The test consists of two or more "sets" of questions, each set concerning a different problem. Typical record keeping problems might involve the organization or collation of data from several sources; scheduling; maintaining a record system using running balances; or completion of a table summarizing data using totals, subtotals, averages and percent's.
3. **Preparing written material** -These questions test for the ability to present information clearly and accurately, and to organize paragraphs logically and comprehensibly. For some questions, you will be given information in two or three sentences followed by four restatements of the information. You must then choose the best version. For other questions, you will be given paragraphs with their sentences out of order. You must then choose, from four suggestions, the best order for the sentences...
4. **Public contact principles and practices** - These questions test for knowledge of techniques used to interact with other people, to gather and present information, and to provide assistance, advice, and effective customer service in a courteous and professional manner. Questions will cover such topics as understanding and responding to people with diverse needs, perspectives, personalities, and levels of familiarity with agency operations, as well as acting in a way that both serves the public and reflects well on your agency.
5. **Supervision** - These questions test for knowledge of the principles and practices employed in planning, organizing, and controlling the activities of a work unit toward predetermined objectives. The concepts covered, usually in a situational question format, include such topics as assigning and reviewing work; evaluating performance; maintaining work standards; motivating and developing subordinates; implementing procedural change; increasing efficiency; and dealing with problems of absenteeism, morale, and discipline.
6. **Understanding and interpreting written material** - These questions test how well you comprehend mitten material. You will be provided with brief reading selections and will be asked questions about the selections. All the information required to answer the questions will be presented in the selections.

HOW TO TAKE A TEST

I. YOU MUST PASS AN EXAMINATION

A. *WHAT EVERY CANDIDATE SHOULD KNOW*

Examination applicants often ask us for help in preparing for the written test. What can I study in advance? What kinds of questions will be asked? How will the test be given? How will the papers be graded?

As an applicant for a civil service examination, you may be wondering about some of these things. Our purpose here is to suggest effective methods of advance study and to describe civil service examinations.

Your chances for success on this examination can be increased if you know how to prepare. Those "pre-examination jitters" can be reduced if you know what to expect. You can even experience an adventure in good citizenship if you know why civil service exams are given.

B. *WHY ARE CIVIL SERVICE EXAMINATIONS GIVEN?*

Civil service examinations are important to you in two ways. As a citizen, you want public jobs filled by employees who know how to do their work. As a job seeker, you want a fair chance to compete for that job on an equal footing with other candidates. The best-known means of accomplishing this two-fold goal is the competitive examination.

Exams are widely publicized throughout the nation. They may be administered for jobs in federal, state, city, municipal, town or village governments or agencies.

Any citizen may apply, with some limitations, such as the age or residence of applicants. Your experience and education may be reviewed to see whether you meet the requirements for the particular examination. When these requirements exist, they are reasonable and applied consistently to all applicants. Thus, a competitive examination may cause you some uneasiness now, but it is your privilege and safeguard.

C. *HOW ARE CIVIL SERVICE EXAMS DEVELOPED?*

Examinations are carefully written by trained technicians who are specialists in the field known as "psychological measurement," in consultation with recognized authorities in the field of work that the test will cover. These experts recommend the subject matter areas or skills to be tested; only those knowledges or skills important to your success on the job are included. The most reliable books and source materials available are used as references. Together, the experts and technicians judge the difficulty level of the questions.

Test technicians know how to phrase questions so that the problem is clearly stated. Their ethics do not permit "trick" or "catch" questions. Questions may have been tried out on sample groups, or subjected to statistical analysis, to determine their usefulness.

Written tests are often used in combination with performance tests, ratings of training and experience, and oral interviews. All of these measures combine to form the best-known means of finding the right person for the right job.

II. HOW TO PASS THE WRITTEN TEST

A. NATURE OF THE EXAMINATION

To prepare intelligently for civil service examinations, you should know how they differ from school examinations you have taken. In school you were assigned certain definite pages to read or subjects to cover. The examination questions were quite detailed and usually emphasized memory. Civil service exams, on the other hand, try to discover your present ability to perform the duties of a position, plus your potentiality to learn these duties. In other words, a civil service exam attempts to predict how successful you will be. Questions cover such a broad area that they cannot be as minute and detailed as school exam questions.

In the public service similar kinds of work, or positions, are grouped together in one "class." This process is known as *position-classification*. All the positions in a class are paid according to the salary range for that class. One class title covers all of these positions, and they are all tested by the same examination.

B. FOUR BASIC STEPS

1) Study the announcement

How, then, can you know what subjects to study? Our best answer is: "Learn as much as possible about the class of positions for which you've applied." The exam will test the knowledge, skills and abilities needed to do the work.

Your most valuable source of information about the position you want is the official exam announcement. This announcement lists the training and experience qualifications. Check these standards and apply only if you come reasonably close to meeting them.

The brief description of the position in the examination announcement offers some clues to the subjects which will be tested. Think about the job itself. Review the duties in your mind. Can you perform them, or are there some in which you are rusty? Fill in the blank spots in your preparation.

Many jurisdictions preview the written test in the exam announcement by including a section called "Knowledge and Abilities Required," "Scope of the Examination," or some similar heading. Here you will find out specifically what fields will be tested.

2) Review your own background

Once you learn in general what the position is all about, and what you need to know to do the work, ask yourself which subjects you already know fairly well and which need improvement. You may wonder whether to concentrate on improving your strong areas or on building some background in your fields of weakness. When the announcement has specified "some knowledge" or "considerable knowledge," or has used adjectives like "beginning principles of..." or "advanced ... methods," you can get a clue as to the number and difficulty of questions to be asked in any given field. More questions, and hence broader coverage, would be included for those subjects which are more important in the work. Now weigh your strengths and weaknesses against the job requirements and prepare accordingly.

3) Determine the level of the position

Another way to tell how intensively you should prepare is to understand the level of the job for which you are applying. Is it the entering level? In other words, is this the position in which beginners in a field of work are hired? Or is it an intermediate or advanced level? Sometimes this is indicated by such words as "Junior" or "Senior" in the class title. Other jurisdictions use Roman numerals to designate the level – Clerk I, Clerk II, for example. The word "Supervisor" sometimes appears in the title. If the level is not indicated by the title, check the description of duties. Will you be working under very close supervision, or will you have responsibility for independent decisions in this work?

4) Choose appropriate study materials

Now that you know the subjects to be examined and the relative amount of each subject to be covered, you can choose suitable study materials. For beginning level jobs, or even advanced ones, if you have a pronounced weakness in some aspect of your training, read a modern, standard textbook in that field. Be sure it is up to date and has general coverage. Such books are normally available at your library, and the librarian will be glad to help you locate one. For entry-level positions, questions of appropriate difficulty are chosen – neither highly advanced questions, nor those too simple. Such questions require careful thought but not advanced training.

If the position for which you are applying is technical or advanced, you will read more advanced, specialized material. If you are already familiar with the basic principles of your field, elementary textbooks would waste your time. Concentrate on advanced textbooks and technical periodicals. Think through the concepts and review difficult problems in your field.

These are all general sources. You can get more ideas on your own initiative, following these leads. For example, training manuals and publications of the government agency which employs workers in your field can be useful, particularly for technical and professional positions. A letter or visit to the government department involved may result in more specific study suggestions, and certainly will provide you with a more definite idea of the exact nature of the position you are seeking.

III. KINDS OF TESTS

Tests are used for purposes other than measuring knowledge and ability to perform specified duties. For some positions, it is equally important to test ability to make adjustments to new situations or to profit from training. In others, basic mental abilities not dependent on information are essential. Questions which test these things may not appear as pertinent to the duties of the position as those which test for knowledge and information. Yet they are often highly important parts of a fair examination. For very general questions, it is almost impossible to help you direct your study efforts. What we can do is to point out some of the more common of these general abilities needed in public service positions and describe some typical questions.

1) General information

Broad, general information has been found useful for predicting job success in some kinds of work. This is tested in a variety of ways, from vocabulary lists to questions about current events. Basic background in some field of work, such as sociology or economics, may be sampled in a group of questions. Often these are principles which have become familiar to most persons through exposure rather than through formal training. It is difficult to advise you how to study for these questions; being alert to the world around you is our best suggestion.

2) Verbal ability

An example of an ability needed in many positions is verbal or language ability. Verbal ability is, in brief, the ability to use and understand words. Vocabulary and grammar tests are typical measures of this ability. Reading comprehension or paragraph interpretation questions are common in many kinds of civil service tests. You are given a paragraph of written material and asked to find its central meaning.

3) Numerical ability

Number skills can be tested by the familiar arithmetic problem, by checking paired lists of numbers to see which are alike and which are different, or by interpreting charts and graphs. In the latter test, a graph may be printed in the test booklet which you are asked to use as the basis for answering questions.

4) Observation

A popular test for law-enforcement positions is the observation test. A picture is shown to you for several minutes, then taken away. Questions about the picture test your ability to observe both details and larger elements.

5) Following directions

In many positions in the public service, the employee must be able to carry out written instructions dependably and accurately. You may be given a chart with several columns, each column listing a variety of information. The questions require you to carry out directions involving the information given in the chart.

6) Skills and aptitudes

Performance tests effectively measure some manual skills and aptitudes. When the skill is one in which you are trained, such as typing or shorthand, you can practice. These tests are often very much like those given in business school or high school courses. For many of the other skills and aptitudes, however, no short-time preparation can be made. Skills and abilities natural to you or that you have developed throughout your lifetime are being tested.

Many of the general questions just described provide all the data needed to answer the questions and ask you to use your reasoning ability to find the answers. Your best preparation for these tests, as well as for tests of facts and ideas, is to be at your physical and mental best. You, no doubt, have your own methods of getting into an exam-taking mood and keeping "in shape." The next section lists some ideas on this subject.

IV. KINDS OF QUESTIONS

Only rarely is the "essay" question, which you answer in narrative form, used in civil service tests. Civil service tests are usually of the short-answer type. Full instructions for answering these questions will be given to you at the examination. But in case this is your first experience with short-answer questions and separate answer sheets, here is what you need to know:

1) Multiple-choice Questions

Most popular of the short-answer questions is the "multiple choice" or "best answer" question. It can be used, for example, to test for factual knowledge, ability to solve problems or judgment in meeting situations found at work.

A multiple-choice question is normally one of three types—
- It can begin with an incomplete statement followed by several possible endings. You are to find the one ending which *best* completes the statement, although some of the others may not be entirely wrong.
- It can also be a complete statement in the form of a question which is answered by choosing one of the statements listed.

- It can be in the form of a problem – again you select the best answer.

Here is an example of a multiple-choice question with a discussion which should give you some clues as to the method for choosing the right answer:

When an employee has a complaint about his assignment, the action which will *best* help him overcome his difficulty is to
- A. discuss his difficulty with his coworkers
- B. take the problem to the head of the organization
- C. take the problem to the person who gave him the assignment
- D. say nothing to anyone about his complaint

In answering this question, you should study each of the choices to find which is best. Consider choice "A" – Certainly an employee may discuss his complaint with fellow employees, but no change or improvement can result, and the complaint remains unresolved. Choice "B" is a poor choice since the head of the organization probably does not know what assignment you have been given, and taking your problem to him is known as "going over the head" of the supervisor. The supervisor, or person who made the assignment, is the person who can clarify it or correct any injustice. Choice "C" is, therefore, correct. To say nothing, as in choice "D," is unwise. Supervisors have and interest in knowing the problems employees are facing, and the employee is seeking a solution to his problem.

2) True/False Questions

The "true/false" or "right/wrong" form of question is sometimes used. Here a complete statement is given. Your job is to decide whether the statement is right or wrong.

SAMPLE: A roaming cell-phone call to a nearby city costs less than a non-roaming call to a distant city.

This statement is wrong, or false, since roaming calls are more expensive.

This is not a complete list of all possible question forms, although most of the others are variations of these common types. You will always get complete directions for answering questions. Be sure you understand *how* to mark your answers – ask questions until you do.

V. RECORDING YOUR ANSWERS

Computer terminals are used more and more today for many different kinds of exams.

For an examination with very few applicants, you may be told to record your answers in the test booklet itself. Separate answer sheets are much more common. If this separate answer sheet is to be scored by machine – and this is often the case – it is highly important that you mark your answers correctly in order to get credit.

An electronic scoring machine is often used in civil service offices because of the speed with which papers can be scored. Machine-scored answer sheets must be marked with a pencil, which will be given to you. This pencil has a high graphite content which responds to the electronic scoring machine. As a matter of fact, stray dots may register as answers, so do not let your pencil rest on the answer sheet while you are pondering the correct answer. Also, if your pencil lead breaks or is otherwise defective, ask for another.

Since the answer sheet will be dropped in a slot in the scoring machine, be careful not to bend the corners or get the paper crumpled.

The answer sheet normally has five vertical columns of numbers, with 30 numbers to a column. These numbers correspond to the question numbers in your test booklet. After each number, going across the page are four or five pairs of dotted lines. These short dotted lines have small letters or numbers above them. The first two pairs may also have a "T" or "F" above the letters. This indicates that the first two pairs only are to be used if the questions are of the true-false type. If the questions are multiple choice, disregard the "T" and "F" and pay attention only to the small letters or numbers.

Answer your questions in the manner of the sample that follows:

32. The largest city in the United States is
    A. Washington, D.C.
    B. New York City
    C. Chicago
    D. Detroit
    E. San Francisco

1) Choose the answer you think is best. (New York City is the largest, so "B" is correct.)
2) Find the row of dotted lines numbered the same as the question you are answering. (Find row number 32)
3) Find the pair of dotted lines corresponding to the answer. (Find the pair of lines under the mark "B.")
4) Make a solid black mark between the dotted lines.

VI. BEFORE THE TEST

Common sense will help you find procedures to follow to get ready for an examination. Too many of us, however, overlook these sensible measures. Indeed, nervousness and fatigue have been found to be the most serious reasons why applicants fail to do their best on civil service tests. Here is a list of reminders:

- Begin your preparation early – Don't wait until the last minute to go scurrying around for books and materials or to find out what the position is all about.
- Prepare continuously – An hour a night for a week is better than an all-night cram session. This has been definitely established. What is more, a night a week for a month will return better dividends than crowding your study into a shorter period of time.
- Locate the place of the exam – You have been sent a notice telling you when and where to report for the examination. If the location is in a different town or otherwise unfamiliar to you, it would be well to inquire the best route and learn something about the building.
- Relax the night before the test – Allow your mind to rest. Do not study at all that night. Plan some mild recreation or diversion; then go to bed early and get a good night's sleep.
- Get up early enough to make a leisurely trip to the place for the test – This way unforeseen events, traffic snarls, unfamiliar buildings, etc. will not upset you.
- Dress comfortably – A written test is not a fashion show. You will be known by number and not by name, so wear something comfortable.

- Leave excess paraphernalia at home – Shopping bags and odd bundles will get in your way. You need bring only the items mentioned in the official notice you received; usually everything you need is provided. Do not bring reference books to the exam. They will only confuse those last minutes and be taken away from you when in the test room.
- Arrive somewhat ahead of time – If because of transportation schedules you must get there very early, bring a newspaper or magazine to take your mind off yourself while waiting.
- Locate the examination room – When you have found the proper room, you will be directed to the seat or part of the room where you will sit. Sometimes you are given a sheet of instructions to read while you are waiting. Do not fill out any forms until you are told to do so; just read them and be prepared.
- Relax and prepare to listen to the instructions
- If you have any physical problem that may keep you from doing your best, be sure to tell the test administrator. If you are sick or in poor health, you really cannot do your best on the exam. You can come back and take the test some other time.

VII. AT THE TEST

The day of the test is here and you have the test booklet in your hand. The temptation to get going is very strong. Caution! There is more to success than knowing the right answers. You must know how to identify your papers and understand variations in the type of short-answer question used in this particular examination. Follow these suggestions for maximum results from your efforts:

1) Cooperate with the monitor

The test administrator has a duty to create a situation in which you can be as much at ease as possible. He will give instructions, tell you when to begin, check to see that you are marking your answer sheet correctly, and so on. He is not there to guard you, although he will see that your competitors do not take unfair advantage. He wants to help you do your best.

2) Listen to all instructions

Don't jump the gun! Wait until you understand all directions. In most civil service tests you get more time than you need to answer the questions. So don't be in a hurry. Read each word of instructions until you clearly understand the meaning. Study the examples, listen to all announcements and follow directions. Ask questions if you do not understand what to do.

3) Identify your papers

Civil service exams are usually identified by number only. You will be assigned a number; you must not put your name on your test papers. Be sure to copy your number correctly. Since more than one exam may be given, copy your exact examination title.

4) Plan your time

Unless you are told that a test is a "speed" or "rate of work" test, speed itself is usually not important. Time enough to answer all the questions will be provided, but this does not mean that you have all day. An overall time limit has been set. Divide the total time (in minutes) by the number of questions to determine the approximate time you have for each question.

5) Do not linger over difficult questions

If you come across a difficult question, mark it with a paper clip (useful to have along) and come back to it when you have been through the booklet. One caution if you do this – be sure to skip a number on your answer sheet as well. Check often to be sure that you have not lost your place and that you are marking in the row numbered the same as the question you are answering.

6) Read the questions

Be sure you know what the question asks! Many capable people are unsuccessful because they failed to *read* the questions correctly.

7) Answer all questions

Unless you have been instructed that a penalty will be deducted for incorrect answers, it is better to guess than to omit a question.

8) Speed tests

It is often better NOT to guess on speed tests. It has been found that on timed tests people are tempted to spend the last few seconds before time is called in marking answers at random – without even reading them – in the hope of picking up a few extra points. To discourage this practice, the instructions may warn you that your score will be "corrected" for guessing. That is, a penalty will be applied. The incorrect answers will be deducted from the correct ones, or some other penalty formula will be used.

9) Review your answers

If you finish before time is called, go back to the questions you guessed or omitted to give them further thought. Review other answers if you have time.

10) Return your test materials

If you are ready to leave before others have finished or time is called, take ALL your materials to the monitor and leave quietly. Never take any test material with you. The monitor can discover whose papers are not complete, and taking a test booklet may be grounds for disqualification.

VIII. EXAMINATION TECHNIQUES

1) Read the general instructions carefully. These are usually printed on the first page of the exam booklet. As a rule, these instructions refer to the timing of the examination; the fact that you should not start work until the signal and must stop work at a signal, etc. If there are any *special* instructions, such as a choice of questions to be answered, make sure that you note this instruction carefully.

2) When you are ready to start work on the examination, that is as soon as the signal has been given, read the instructions to each question booklet, underline any key words or phrases, such as *least, best, outline, describe* and the like. In this way you will tend to answer as requested rather than discover on reviewing your paper that you *listed without describing*, that you selected the *worst* choice rather than the *best* choice, etc.

3) If the examination is of the objective or multiple-choice type – that is, each question will also give a series of possible answers: A, B, C or D, and you are called upon to select the best answer and write the letter next to that answer on your answer paper – it is advisable to start answering each question in turn. There may be anywhere from 50 to 100 such questions in the three or four hours allotted and you can see how much time would be taken if you read through all the questions before beginning to answer any. Furthermore, if you come across a question or group of questions which you know would be difficult to answer, it would undoubtedly affect your handling of all the other questions.

4) If the examination is of the essay type and contains but a few questions, it is a moot point as to whether you should read all the questions before starting to answer any one. Of course, if you are given a choice – say five out of seven and the like – then it is essential to read all the questions so you can eliminate the two that are most difficult. If, however, you are asked to answer all the questions, there may be danger in trying to answer the easiest one first because you may find that you will spend too much time on it. The best technique is to answer the first question, then proceed to the second, etc.

5) Time your answers. Before the exam begins, write down the time it started, then add the time allowed for the examination and write down the time it must be completed, then divide the time available somewhat as follows:
    - If 3-1/2 hours are allowed, that would be 210 minutes. If you have 80 objective-type questions, that would be an average of 2-1/2 minutes per question. Allow yourself no more than 2 minutes per question, or a total of 160 minutes, which will permit about 50 minutes to review.
    - If for the time allotment of 210 minutes there are 7 essay questions to answer, that would average about 30 minutes a question. Give yourself only 25 minutes per question so that you have about 35 minutes to review.

6) The most important instruction is to *read each question* and make sure you know what is wanted. The second most important instruction is to *time yourself properly* so that you answer every question. The third most important instruction is to *answer every question*. Guess if you have to but include something for each question. Remember that you will receive no credit for a blank and will probably receive some credit if you write something in answer to an essay question. If you guess a letter – say "B" for a multiple-choice question – you may have guessed right. If you leave a blank as an answer to a multiple-choice question, the examiners may respect your feelings but it will not add a point to your score. Some exams may penalize you for wrong answers, so in such cases *only*, you may not want to guess unless you have some basis for your answer.

7) Suggestions
    a. Objective-type questions
        1. Examine the question booklet for proper sequence of pages and questions
        2. Read all instructions carefully
        3. Skip any question which seems too difficult; return to it after all other questions have been answered
        4. Apportion your time properly; do not spend too much time on any single question or group of questions

5. Note and underline key words – *all, most, fewest, least, best, worst, same, opposite*, etc.
6. Pay particular attention to negatives
7. Note unusual option, e.g., unduly long, short, complex, different or similar in content to the body of the question
8. Observe the use of "hedging" words – *probably, may, most likely*, etc.
9. Make sure that your answer is put next to the same number as the question
10. Do not second-guess unless you have good reason to believe the second answer is definitely more correct
11. Cross out original answer if you decide another answer is more accurate; do not erase until you are ready to hand your paper in
12. Answer all questions; guess unless instructed otherwise
13. Leave time for review

b. Essay questions
1. Read each question carefully
2. Determine exactly what is wanted. Underline key words or phrases.
3. Decide on outline or paragraph answer
4. Include many different points and elements unless asked to develop any one or two points or elements
5. Show impartiality by giving pros and cons unless directed to select one side only
6. Make and write down any assumptions you find necessary to answer the questions
7. Watch your English, grammar, punctuation and choice of words
8. Time your answers; don't crowd material

8) Answering the essay question

Most essay questions can be answered by framing the specific response around several key words or ideas. Here are a few such key words or ideas:

M's: manpower, materials, methods, money, management
P's: purpose, program, policy, plan, procedure, practice, problems, pitfalls, personnel, public relations

a. Six basic steps in handling problems:
1. Preliminary plan and background development
2. Collect information, data and facts
3. Analyze and interpret information, data and facts
4. Analyze and develop solutions as well as make recommendations
5. Prepare report and sell recommendations
6. Install recommendations and follow up effectiveness

b. Pitfalls to avoid
1. *Taking things for granted* – A statement of the situation does not necessarily imply that each of the elements is necessarily true; for example, a complaint may be invalid and biased so that all that can be taken for granted is that a complaint has been registered

2. *Considering only one side of a situation* – Wherever possible, indicate several alternatives and then point out the reasons you selected the best one
3. *Failing to indicate follow up* – Whenever your answer indicates action on your part, make certain that you will take proper follow-up action to see how successful your recommendations, procedures or actions turn out to be
4. *Taking too long in answering any single question* – Remember to time your answers properly

IX. AFTER THE TEST

Scoring procedures differ in detail among civil service jurisdictions although the general principles are the same. Whether the papers are hand-scored or graded by machine we have described, they are nearly always graded by number. That is, the person who marks the paper knows only the number – never the name – of the applicant. Not until all the papers have been graded will they be matched with names. If other tests, such as training and experience or oral interview ratings have been given, scores will be combined. Different parts of the examination usually have different weights. For example, the written test might count 60 percent of the final grade, and a rating of training and experience 40 percent. In many jurisdictions, veterans will have a certain number of points added to their grades.

After the final grade has been determined, the names are placed in grade order and an eligible list is established. There are various methods for resolving ties between those who get the same final grade – probably the most common is to place first the name of the person whose application was received first. Job offers are made from the eligible list in the order the names appear on it. You will be notified of your grade and your rank as soon as all these computations have been made. This will be done as rapidly as possible.

People who are found to meet the requirements in the announcement are called "eligibles." Their names are put on a list of eligible candidates. An eligible's chances of getting a job depend on how high he stands on this list and how fast agencies are filling jobs from the list.

When a job is to be filled from a list of eligibles, the agency asks for the names of people on the list of eligibles for that job. When the civil service commission receives this request, it sends to the agency the names of the three people highest on this list. Or, if the job to be filled has specialized requirements, the office sends the agency the names of the top three persons who meet these requirements from the general list.

The appointing officer makes a choice from among the three people whose names were sent to him. If the selected person accepts the appointment, the names of the others are put back on the list to be considered for future openings.

That is the rule in hiring from all kinds of eligible lists, whether they are for typist, carpenter, chemist, or something else. For every vacancy, the appointing officer has his choice of any one of the top three eligibles on the list. This explains why the person whose name is on top of the list sometimes does not get an appointment when some of the persons lower on the list do. If the appointing officer chooses the second or third eligible, the No. 1 eligible does not get a job at once, but stays on the list until he is appointed or the list is terminated.

X. HOW TO PASS THE INTERVIEW TEST

The examination for which you applied requires an oral interview test. You have already taken the written test and you are now being called for the interview test – the final part of the formal examination.

You may think that it is not possible to prepare for an interview test and that there are no procedures to follow during an interview. Our purpose is to point out some things you can do in advance that will help you and some good rules to follow and pitfalls to avoid while you are being interviewed.

What is an interview supposed to test?

The written examination is designed to test the technical knowledge and competence of the candidate; the oral is designed to evaluate intangible qualities, not readily measured otherwise, and to establish a list showing the relative fitness of each candidate – as measured against his competitors – for the position sought. Scoring is not on the basis of "right" and "wrong," but on a sliding scale of values ranging from "not passable" to "outstanding." As a matter of fact, it is possible to achieve a relatively low score without a single "incorrect" answer because of evident weakness in the qualities being measured.

Occasionally, an examination may consist entirely of an oral test – either an individual or a group oral. In such cases, information is sought concerning the technical knowledges and abilities of the candidate, since there has been no written examination for this purpose. More commonly, however, an oral test is used to supplement a written examination.

Who conducts interviews?

The composition of oral boards varies among different jurisdictions. In nearly all, a representative of the personnel department serves as chairman. One of the members of the board may be a representative of the department in which the candidate would work. In some cases, "outside experts" are used, and, frequently, a businessman or some other representative of the general public is asked to serve. Labor and management or other special groups may be represented. The aim is to secure the services of experts in the appropriate field.

However the board is composed, it is a good idea (and not at all improper or unethical) to ascertain in advance of the interview who the members are and what groups they represent. When you are introduced to them, you will have some idea of their backgrounds and interests, and at least you will not stutter and stammer over their names.

What should be done before the interview?

While knowledge about the board members is useful and takes some of the surprise element out of the interview, there is other preparation which is more substantive. It *is* possible to prepare for an oral interview – in several ways:

1) Keep a copy of your application and review it carefully before the interview

This may be the only document before the oral board, and the starting point of the interview. Know what education and experience you have listed there, and the sequence and dates of all of it. Sometimes the board will ask you to review the highlights of your experience for them; you should not have to hem and haw doing it.

2) Study the class specification and the examination announcement

Usually, the oral board has one or both of these to guide them. The qualities, characteristics or knowledges required by the position sought are stated in these documents. They offer valuable clues as to the nature of the oral interview. For example, if the job involves supervisory responsibilities, the announcement will usually indicate that knowledge of modern supervisory methods and the qualifications of the candidate as a supervisor will be tested. If so, you can expect such questions, frequently in the form of a hypothetical situation which you are expected to solve. NEVER go into an oral without knowledge of the duties and responsibilities of the job you seek.

3) Think through each qualification required

Try to visualize the kind of questions you would ask if you were a board member. How well could you answer them? Try especially to appraise your own knowledge and background in each area, *measured against the job sought*, and identify any areas in which you are weak. Be critical and realistic – do not flatter yourself.

4) Do some general reading in areas in which you feel you may be weak

For example, if the job involves supervision and your past experience has NOT, some general reading in supervisory methods and practices, particularly in the field of human relations, might be useful. Do NOT study agency procedures or detailed manuals. The oral board will be testing your understanding and capacity, not your memory.

5) Get a good night's sleep and watch your general health and mental attitude

You will want a clear head at the interview. Take care of a cold or any other minor ailment, and of course, no hangovers.

What should be done on the day of the interview?

Now comes the day of the interview itself. Give yourself plenty of time to get there. Plan to arrive somewhat ahead of the scheduled time, particularly if your appointment is in the fore part of the day. If a previous candidate fails to appear, the board might be ready for you a bit early. By early afternoon an oral board is almost invariably behind schedule if there are many candidates, and you may have to wait. Take along a book or magazine to read, or your application to review, but leave any extraneous material in the waiting room when you go in for your interview. In any event, relax and compose yourself.

The matter of dress is important. The board is forming impressions about you – from your experience, your manners, your attitude, and your appearance. Give your personal appearance careful attention. Dress your best, but not your flashiest. Choose conservative, appropriate clothing, and be sure it is immaculate. This is a business interview, and your appearance should indicate that you regard it as such. Besides, being well groomed and properly dressed will help boost your confidence.

Sooner or later, someone will call your name and escort you into the interview room. *This is it.* From here on you are on your own. It is too late for any more preparation. But remember, you asked for this opportunity to prove your fitness, and you are here because your request was granted.

What happens when you go in?

The usual sequence of events will be as follows: The clerk (who is often the board stenographer) will introduce you to the chairman of the oral board, who will introduce you to the other members of the board. Acknowledge the introductions before you sit down. Do not be surprised if you find a microphone facing you or a stenotypist sitting by. Oral interviews are usually recorded in the event of an appeal or other review.

Usually the chairman of the board will open the interview by reviewing the highlights of your education and work experience from your application – primarily for the benefit of the other members of the board, as well as to get the material into the record. Do not interrupt or comment unless there is an error or significant misinterpretation; if that is the case, do not hesitate. But do not quibble about insignificant matters. Also, he will usually ask you some question about your education, experience or your present job – partly to get you to start talking and to establish the interviewing "rapport." He may start the actual questioning, or turn it over to one of the other members. Frequently, each member undertakes the questioning on a particular area, one in which he is perhaps most competent, so you can expect each member to participate in the examination. Because time is limited, you may also expect some rather abrupt switches in the direction the questioning takes, so do not be upset by it. Normally, a board member will not pursue a single line of questioning unless he discovers a particular strength or weakness.

After each member has participated, the chairman will usually ask whether any member has any further questions, then will ask you if you have anything you wish to add. Unless you are expecting this question, it may floor you. Worse, it may start you off on an extended, extemporaneous speech. The board is not usually seeking more information. The question is principally to offer you a last opportunity to present further qualifications or to indicate that you have nothing to add. So, if you feel that a significant qualification or characteristic has been overlooked, it is proper to point it out in a sentence or so. Do not compliment the board on the thoroughness of their examination – they have been sketchy, and you know it. If you wish, merely say, "No thank you, I have nothing further to add." This is a point where you can "talk yourself out" of a good impression or fail to present an important bit of information. Remember, *you close the interview yourself*.

The chairman will then say, "That is all, Mr. _____, thank you." Do not be startled; the interview is over, and quicker than you think. Thank him, gather your belongings and take your leave. Save your sigh of relief for the other side of the door.

How to put your best foot forward

Throughout this entire process, you may feel that the board individually and collectively is trying to pierce your defenses, seek out your hidden weaknesses and embarrass and confuse you. Actually, this is not true. They are obliged to make an appraisal of your qualifications for the job you are seeking, and they want to see you in your best light. Remember, they must interview all candidates and a non-cooperative candidate may become a failure in spite of their best efforts to bring out his qualifications. Here are 15 suggestions that will help you:

1) Be natural – Keep your attitude confident, not cocky

If you are not confident that you can do the job, do not expect the board to be. Do not apologize for your weaknesses, try to bring out your strong points. The board is interested in a positive, not negative, presentation. Cockiness will antagonize any board member and make him wonder if you are covering up a weakness by a false show of strength.

2) Get comfortable, but don't lounge or sprawl

Sit erectly but not stiffly. A careless posture may lead the board to conclude that you are careless in other things, or at least that you are not impressed by the importance of the occasion. Either conclusion is natural, even if incorrect. Do not fuss with your clothing, a pencil or an ashtray. Your hands may occasionally be useful to emphasize a point; do not let them become a point of distraction.

3) Do not wisecrack or make small talk

This is a serious situation, and your attitude should show that you consider it as such. Further, the time of the board is limited – they do not want to waste it, and neither should you.

4) Do not exaggerate your experience or abilities

In the first place, from information in the application or other interviews and sources, the board may know more about you than you think. Secondly, you probably will not get away with it. An experienced board is rather adept at spotting such a situation, so do not take the chance.

5) If you know a board member, do not make a point of it, yet do not hide it

Certainly you are not fooling him, and probably not the other members of the board. Do not try to take advantage of your acquaintanceship – it will probably do you little good.

6) Do not dominate the interview

Let the board do that. They will give you the clues – do not assume that you have to do all the talking. Realize that the board has a number of questions to ask you, and do not try to take up all the interview time by showing off your extensive knowledge of the answer to the first one.

7) Be attentive

You only have 20 minutes or so, and you should keep your attention at its sharpest throughout. When a member is addressing a problem or question to you, give him your undivided attention. Address your reply principally to him, but do not exclude the other board members.

8) Do not interrupt

A board member may be stating a problem for you to analyze. He will ask you a question when the time comes. Let him state the problem, and wait for the question.

9) Make sure you understand the question

Do not try to answer until you are sure what the question is. If it is not clear, restate it in your own words or ask the board member to clarify it for you. However, do not haggle about minor elements.

10) Reply promptly but not hastily

A common entry on oral board rating sheets is "candidate responded readily," or "candidate hesitated in replies." Respond as promptly and quickly as you can, but do not jump to a hasty, ill-considered answer.

11) Do not be peremptory in your answers

A brief answer is proper – but do not fire your answer back. That is a losing game from your point of view. The board member can probably ask questions much faster than you can answer them.

12) Do not try to create the answer you think the board member wants

He is interested in what kind of mind you have and how it works – not in playing games. Furthermore, he can usually spot this practice and will actually grade you down on it.

13) Do not switch sides in your reply merely to agree with a board member

Frequently, a member will take a contrary position merely to draw you out and to see if you are willing and able to defend your point of view. Do not start a debate, yet do not surrender a good position. If a position is worth taking, it is worth defending.

14) Do not be afraid to admit an error in judgment if you are shown to be wrong

The board knows that you are forced to reply without any opportunity for careful consideration. Your answer may be demonstrably wrong. If so, admit it and get on with the interview.

15) Do not dwell at length on your present job

The opening question may relate to your present assignment. Answer the question but do not go into an extended discussion. You are being examined for a *new* job, not your present one. As a matter of fact, try to phrase ALL your answers in terms of the job for which you are being examined.

Basis of Rating

Probably you will forget most of these "do's" and "don'ts" when you walk into the oral interview room. Even remembering them all will not ensure you a passing grade. Perhaps you did not have the qualifications in the first place. But remembering them will help you to put your best foot forward, without treading on the toes of the board members.

Rumor and popular opinion to the contrary notwithstanding, an oral board wants you to make the best appearance possible. They know you are under pressure – but they also want to see how you respond to it as a guide to what your reaction would be under the pressures of the job you seek. They will be influenced by the degree of poise you display, the personal traits you show and the manner in which you respond.

ABOUT THIS BOOK

This book contains tests divided into Examination Sections. Go through each test, answering every question in the margin. We have also attached a sample answer sheet at the back of the book that can be removed and used. At the end of each test look at the answer key and check your answers. On the ones you got wrong, look at the right answer choice and learn. Do not fill in the answers first. Do not memorize the questions and answers, but understand the answer and principles involved. On your test, the questions will likely be different from the samples. Questions are changed and new ones added. If you understand these past questions you should have success with any changes that arise. Tests may consist of several types of questions. We have additional books on each subject should more study be advisable or necessary for you. Finally, the more you study, the better prepared you will be. This book is intended to be the last thing you study before you walk into the examination room. Prior study of relevant texts is also recommended. NLC publishes some of these in our Fundamental Series. Knowledge and good sense are important factors in passing your exam. Good luck also helps. So now study this Passbook, absorb the material contained within and take that knowledge into the examination. Then do your best to pass that exam.

EXAMINATION SECTION

EXAMINATION SECTION
TEST 1

DIRECTIONS: Each question or incomplete statement is followed by several suggested answers or completions. Select the one that BEST answers the question or completes the statement. *PRINT THE LETTER OF THE CORRECT ANSWER IN THE SPACE AT THE RIGHT.*

1. A certain system for handling office supplies requires that supplies be issued to the various agency offices only on a bi-weekly basis and that all supply requisitions be authorized by the unit supervisor.
   The BEST reason for establishing this supplies system is to
   A. standardize ordering descriptions and stock identification codes
   B. prevent the disordering of stock shelves and cabinets by unauthorized persons searching for supplies
   C. ensure that unit supervisors properly exercise their right to make determinations on supply orders
   D. encourage proper utilization of supplies to control the workload

   1.____

2. It is important that every office have a retention and disposal program for filing material. Suppose that you have been appointed administrative assistant in an office with a poorly organized records-retention program.
   In establishing a revised program for the transfer or disposal of records, the step which would logically be taken THIRD in the process is
   A. preparing a safe and inexpensive storage area and setting up an indexing system for records already in storage
   B. determining what papers to retain and for how long a period
   C. taking an inventory of what is filed, where it is filed, how much is filed, and how often it is used
   D. moving records from active to inactive files and destroying useless records

   2.____

3. In the effective design of office forms, the FIRST step to take is to
   A. decide what information should be included
   B. decide the purpose for which the form will be used
   C. identify the form by name and number
   D. identify the employees who will be using the form

   3.____

4. Some designers of office forms prefer to locate the instructions on how to fill out the form at the bottom of it.
   The MOST logical objection to placing such instructions at the bottom of the form is that
   A. instructions at the bottom require an excess of space
   B. all form instructions should be outlined with a separate paragraph
   C. the form may be partly filled out before the instructions are seen
   D. the bottom of the form should be reserved only for authorization and signature

   4.____

5. A formal business report may consist of many parts, including the following:
   I. Table of Contents
   II. List of References
   III. Preface
   IV. Index
   V. List of Tables
   VI. Conclusions or Recommendations

   Of the following, in setting up a formal report, the PROPER order of the six parts listed is
   A. I, III, VI, V, II, IV
   B. IV, III, II, V, VI, I
   C. III, I, V, VI, II, IV
   D. II, V, III, I, IV, VI

6. Three of the basic functions of office management are considered to be planning, controlling, and organizing.
   Of the following, the one which might BEST be considered ORGANIZING activity is
   A. assigning personnel and materials to work units to achieve agreed-upon objectives
   B. determining future objectives and indicating conditions affecting the accomplishment of the goals
   C. evaluating accomplishments and applying necessary corrective measures to insure results
   D. motivating employees to perform their work in accordance with objectives

7. The following four statements relate to office layout.
   I. Position supervisors' desks at the front of their work group so that they can easily be recognized as persons in authority.
   II. Arrange file cabinets and frequently used equipment near the employees who utilize them most often.
   III. Locate the receptionist's desk near the entrance of the office so that visitor traffic will not distract other workers.
   IV. Divide a large office area into many smaller offices by using stationary partitions so that all employees may have privacy and prestige.

   According to authorities in office management and administration, which of these statements are generally recommended guides to effective office layout?
   A. I, II, III   B. II, III, IV   C. II, III   D. All of the above

8. For which of the following purposes would a flow chart have the GREATEST applicability?
   A. Training new employees in performance of routine duties
   B. Determining adequacy of performance of employees
   C. Determining the accuracy of the organization chart
   D. Locating causes of delays in carrying out an operation

9. Office work management concerns tangible accomplishment or production. It has to do with results; it does not deal with the amount of energy expended by the individual who produces the results.
   According to this statement, the production in which of the following kinds of jobs would be MOST difficult to measure accurately?

A(n)
- A. file clerk
- B. secretary
- C. computer operator
- D. office administrator

10. The FIRST step in the statistical analysis of a great mass of data secured from a survey is to
    - A. scan the data to determine which is atypical of the survey
    - B. determine the number of deviations from the average
    - C. arrange the data into groups on the basis of likenesses and differences
    - D. plot the drama on a graph to determine trends

11. Suppose that, as an administrative assistant in charge of an office, you are required to change the layout of your office to accommodate expanding functions.
    The LEAST important factor to be considered in planning the revised layout is the
    - A. relative productivity of individuals in the office
    - B. communication and work flow needs
    - C. need for screening confidential activities from unauthorized persons
    - D. areas of noise concentration

12. Suppose you have instructed a new employee to follow a standardized series of steps to accomplish a job. He is to use a rubber stamp, then a red pencil on the first paper, and a numbering machine on the second. Then, he is to staple the two sheets of paper together and put them to one side. You observe, however, that he sometimes uses the red pencil first, sometimes the numbering machine first. At other times, he does the stapling before using the numbering machine.
    For you as supervisor to suggest that the clerk use the standardized method when doing this job would be
    - A. *bad*, because the clerk should be given a chance to use his independent judgment on the best way to do his job
    - B. *good*, because the clerk's sequence of actions results in a loss of efficiency
    - C. *bad*, because it is not wise to interrupt the work habit the clerk has already developed
    - D. *good*, because the clerk should not be permitted to make unauthorized changes in standard office routines

13. Suppose study of the current records management system for students' transcripts reveals needless recopying of transcript data throughout various offices within the university. On this basis, a recommendation is made that this unnecessary recopying of information be eliminated.
    This decision to eliminate waste in material, time, and space is an application of the office management principle of
    - A. work simplification
    - B. routing and scheduling
    - C. job analysis
    - D. cost and budgetary control

14. It is generally LEAST practical for an office manager to prepare for known peak work periods by
    A. putting job procedures into writing so that they can be handled by more than one person
    B. arranging to make assignments of work on a short-interval scheduling basis
    C. cleaning up as much work as possible ahead of known peak periods
    D. rotating jobs and assignments among different employees to assure staff flexibility

15. The four statements below are about office manuals used for various purposes. If you had the job of designing and controlling several kinds of office manuals to be used in your agency, which one of these statements would BEST apply as a general rule for you to follow?
    A. Office manual content should be classified into main topics with proper subdivisions arranged in strict alphabetical order.
    B. Manual additions and revisions should be distributed promptly to all holders of manuals for their approval, correction, and criticism.
    C. The language used in office manuals should be simple, and charts and diagrams should be interspersed within the narrative material for further clarity.
    D. Office manual content should be classified into main topics arranged in strict alphabetical order with subtopics in sequence according to importance.

16. Suppose that, as an administrative assistant, you have been assigned to plan the reorganization of an office which has not been operating efficiently because of the uncoordinated manner in which new functions have been assigned to it over the past year.
    The FIRST thing you should so is
    A. call a meeting of the office staff and explain the purposes of the planned reorganization
    B. make a cost-value analysis of the present operations to determine what should be changed or eliminated
    C. prepare a diagram of the flow of work as you think it should be
    D. define carefully the current objectives to be achieved by this reorganization

17. Effective organization requires that specific actions be taken in proper sequence. The following are four actions essential to effective organization:
    I. Group activities on the basis of human and material resources
    II. Coordinate functions and provide for good communications
    III. Formulate objectives, policies, and plans
    IV. Determine activities necessary to accomplish goals

    The PROPER sequence of these four actions is:
    A. III, II, IV, I   B. IV, III, I, II   C. III, IV, I, II   D. IV, I, III, II

18. For an administrative assistant to give each of his subordinates exactly the same type of supervision is
    A. *advisable*, because he will gain a reputation for being fair and impartial
    B. *inadvisable*, because subordinates work more diligently when they think they are receiving preferential treatment
    C. *advisable*, because most human problems can be classified into categories which make them easier to handle
    D. *inadvisable*, because people differ and there is no one supervisory procedure that applies in every case to dealing with individuals

19. Suppose that, as an administrative assistant, you find that some of your subordinates are coming to you with complaints you think are trivial.
    For you to hear them through is
    A. *poor practice*; subordinates should be trained to come to you only with major grievances
    B. *good practice*; major grievances sometimes are the underlying cause of minor complaints
    C. *poor practice*; you should delegate this kind of matter and spend your time on more important problems
    D. *good practice*; this will make you more popular with your subordinates

20. Suppose that a new departmental policy has just been established which you feel may be resented by your subordinates, but which they must understand and follow.
    Which would it be MOST advisable for you as their supervisory to do FIRST?
    A. Make clear to your subordinates that you are not responsible for making this policy.
    B. Tell your subordinates that you agree with the policy whether you do or not.
    C. Explain specifically to your subordinates the reasons for the policy and how it is going to affect them.
    D. Distribute a memo outlining the new policy and require your subordinates to read it.

21. An office assistant under your supervision tells you that she is reluctant to speak to one of her subordinates about poor work habits because this subordinate is strong-willed, and she does not want to antagonize her.
    For you to refuse the office assistant's request that you speak to her subordinate about this matter is
    A. *inadvisable*, since you are in a position of greater authority
    B. *advisable*, since supervision of his subordinate is a basic responsibility of that office assistant
    C. *inadvisable*, since the office assistant must work more closely with her subordinate than you do
    D. *advisable*, since you should not risk antagonizing her subordinate yourself

22. The GREATEST advantage to a supervisor of using oral communication as compared to written is the
    A. opportunity provided for immediate feedback
    B. speed with which orders can be given and carried out
    C. reduction in amount of paper work
    D. establishment of an informal atmosphere

23. Of the following, the MOST important reason for an administrative assistant to have private, face-to-face discussions with subordinates about their performance is
    A. encourage a more competitive spirit among employees
    B. give special praise to employees who perform well
    C. discipline employees who perform poorly
    D. help employees improve their work

24. For a supervisor to keep records of reprimands to subordinates about violations of rules is
    A. *poor practice*; such records are evidence of the supervisor's inability to maintain discipline
    B. *good practice*; these records are valuable to support disciplinary actions recommended or taken
    C. *poor practice*; the best way to prevent recurrences is to apply penalties without delay
    D. *good practice*; such records are evidence that the supervisor is doing a good job

25. As an administrative assistant supervising a small office, you decide to hold a staff meeting to try to find an acceptable solution to s problem that is causing serious conflicts within the group.
    At this meeting, your role should be to prevent the problem and
    A. see that the group keeps the problem in focus and does not discuss irrelevant matters
    B. act as chairman of the meeting, but take no other part in the discussion
    C. see to it that each member of the group offers a suggestion for its solution
    D. state you views on the matter before any discussion gets under way

KEY (CORRECT ANSWERS)

1.	D	11.	A
2.	A	12.	B
3.	B	13.	A
4.	C	14.	B
5.	C	15.	C
6.	A	16.	D
7.	C	17.	C
8.	D	18.	D
9.	D	19.	B
10.	C	20.	C

21. B
22. A
23. D
24. B
25. A

TEST 2

DIRECTIONS: Each question or incomplete statement is followed by several suggested answers or completions. Select the one that BEST answers the question or completes the statement. *PRINT THE LETTER OF THE CORRECT ANSWER IN THE SPACE AT THE RIGHT.*

1. Suppose that one of your subordinates who supervises two young office assistants has been late for work a number of times and you have decided to talk to him about it.
   In your discussion, it would be MOST constructive for you to emphasize that
   A. personal problems cannot be used as an excuse for these latenesses
   B. the department suffers financially when he is late
   C. you will be forced to give him a less desirable assignment if his latenesses continue
   D. his latnesses set a bad example to those he supervises

   1.____

2. Suppose that, as a newly-appointed administrative assistant, you are in charge of a small but very busy office. Your four subordinates are often required to make quick decisions on a wide range of matters while answering telephone or in-person inquiries.
   You can MOST efficiently help your subordinates meet such situations by
   A. delegating authority to make such decisions to only one or two trusted subordinates
   B. training each subordinate in the proper response for each kind of inquiry that might be made
   C. making certain that subordinates understand clearly the basic policies that affect these decisions
   D. making each subordinate an expert in one area

   2.____

3. Of the following, the MOST recent development in methods of training supervisors that involves the human relations approach is
   A. conference training   B. the lecture method
   C. the case method   D. sensitivity training

   3.____

4. Which of the following is MOST likely to result in failure as a supervisor?
   A. Showing permissiveness in relations with subordinates
   B. Avoiding delegation of tasks to subordinates
   C. Setting high performance standards for subordinates
   D. Using discipline only when necessary

   4.____

5. The MOST important long-range benefit to an organization of proper delegation of work by supervisors is generally that
   A. subordinates will be developed to assume greater responsibilities
   B. subordinates will perform the work as their supervisors would
   C. errors in delegated work will be eliminated
   D. more efficient communication among organizational components will result

   5.____

6. Which of the following duties would it be LEAST appropriate for an administrative assistant in charge of an office to delegate to an immediate subordinate?
    A. Checking of figures to be used in a report to the head of the department
    B. On-the-job training of newly appointed college office assistants
    C. Reorganization of assignments for higher level office staff
    D. Contacting other school offices for needed information

7. Decisions should be delegated to the lowest point in the organization at which they can be made effectively.
The one of the following which is MOST likely to be a result of the application of this accepted management principle is that
    A. upward communications will be facilitated
    B. potential for more rapid decisions and implementation is increased
    C. coordination of decisions that are made will be simplified
    D. no important factors will be overlooked in making decisions

8. The lecture-demonstration method would be LEAST desirable in a training program set up for
    A. changing the attitudes of long-term employees
    B. informing subordinates about new procedures
    C. explaining how a new office machine works
    D. orientation of new employees

9. Which one of the following conditions would be LEAST likely to indicate a need for employee training?
    A. Large number of employee suggestions
    B. Large amount of overtime
    C. High number of chronic latenesses
    D. Low employee morale

10. An administrative assistant is planning to make a recommendation to change a procedure which would substantially affect the work of his subordinates. For this supervisor to consult with his subordinates about the recommendation before sending it through would be
    A. *undesirable*; subordinates may lose respect for a supervisor who evidences such indecisiveness
    B. *desirable*; since the change in procedure would affect their work, subordinates should decide whether the change should be made
    C. *undesirable*; since subordinates would not receive credit if the procedure were changed, their morale would be lowered
    D. *desirable*; the subordinates may have some worthwhile suggestions concerning the recommendation

11. The BEST way to measure improvement in a selected group of office assistants who have undergone a training course in the use of specific techniques is to
    A. have the trainees fill out questionnaires at the completion of the course as to what they have learned and giving their opinions as to the value of the course

B. compare the performance of the trainees who completed the course with the performance of office assistants who did not take the course
C. compare the performance of the trainees in these techniques before and after the training course
D. compare the degree of success on the next promotion examination of trainees and non-trainees

12. When an administrative assistant finds it necessary to call in a subordinate for a disciplinary interview, his MAIN objective should be to
    A. use techniques which can penetrate any deception and get at the truth
    B. stress correction of, rather than punishment for, past errors
    C. maintain a reputation for being an understanding superior
    D. decide on disciplinary action that is consistent with penalties applied for similar infractions

12._____

13. Suppose that a newly promoted office assistant does satisfactory work during the first five months of her probationary period. However, her supervisor notices shortly after this time that her performance is falling below acceptable standards. The supervisor decides to keep records of this employee's performance, and if there is no significant improvement by the end of 11 months, to recommend that this employee not be given tenure in the higher title.
    This, as the sole course of action, is
    A. *justified*; employees who do not perform satisfactorily should not be promoted
    B. *unjustified*; the supervisor should attempt to determine the cause of the poor performance as soon as possible
    C. *justified*; the supervisor will have given the subordinate the full probationary period to improve herself
    D. *unjustified*; the subordinate should be demoted to her previous title as soon as her work becomes unsatisfactory

13._____

14. Suppose that you are conducting a conference-style training course for a group of 12 office assistants. Miss Jones is the only conferee who has not become involved in the discussion.
    The BEST method of getting Miss Jones to participate is to
    A. ask her to comment on remarks made by the best-informed participant
    B. ask her to give a brief talk at the next session on a topic that interests her
    C. set up a role-play situation and assign her to take a part
    D. ask her a direct questions which you know she can answer

14._____

15. Which of the following is NOT part of the *control* function of office management?
    A. Deciding on alternative courses of action
    B. Reporting periodically on productivity
    C. Evaluating performance against the standards
    D. Correcting deviations when required

15._____

16. Which of the following is NOT a principal aspect of the process of delegation? 16.____
    A. Developing improvements in methods used to carry out assignments
    B. Granting of permission to do what is necessary to carry out assignments
    C. Assignment of duties by a supervisor to an immediate subordinate
    D. Obligation on the part of a subordinate to carry out his assignment

17. Reluctance of a supervisor to delegate work effectively may be due to any or 17.____
    all of the following EXCEPT the supervisor's
    A. unwillingness to take calculated risks
    B. lack of confidence in subordinates
    C. inability to give proper directions as to what he wants done
    D. retention of ultimate responsibility for delegated work

18. A man cannot serve two masters. 18.____
    This statement emphasizes the importance in an organization of following the principle of
    A. specialization of work   B. unity of command
    C. uniformity of assignment   D. span of control

19. In general, the number of subordinates an administrative assistant can 19.____
    supervise effectively tends to vary
    A. *directly* with both similarity and complexity of their duties
    B. *directly* with similarity of their duties and *inversely* with complexity of their duties
    C. *inversely* with both similarity and complex of their duties
    D. *inversely* with similarity of their duties and *directly* with complexity of their duties

20. When an administrative assistant practices *general* rather than *close* 20.____
    supervision, which one of the following is MOST likely to happen?
    A. His subordinates will not be as well-trained as employees who are supervised more closely.
    B. Standards are likely to be lowered because subordinates will be under pressures and will not be motivated to work toward set goals.
    C. He will give fewer specific orders and spend more time on planning and coordinating than those supervisors who practice close supervision.
    D. This supervisor will spend more time checking and correcting mistakes made by subordinates than would one who supervises closely.

Questions 21-25.

DIRECTIONS: Questions 21 through 25 are to be answered SOLELY on the basis of the information contained in the following paragraph.

Since an organization chart is pictorial in nature, there is a tendency for it to be drawn in an artistically balanced and appealing fashion, regardless of the realities of actual organizational structure. In addition to being subject to this distortion, there is the difficulty of communicating in any organization chart the relative importance or the relative size of various component parts of an organizational structure. Furthermore, because of the need for simplicity of design, an organization chart can never indicate the full extent of the interrelationships among the component parts of an organization. These interrelationships are often just as vital as the specifications which an organization chart endeavors to indicate. Yet, if an organization chart were to be drawn with all the wide variety of criss-crossing communication and cooperation networks existent within a typical organization, the chart would probably be much more confusing than informative. It is also obvious that no organization chart as such can "prove" or "disprove" that the organizational structure it represents is effective in realizing the objectives of the organization. At best, an organization chart can only illustrate some of the various factors to be taken into consideration in understanding, devising, or altering organizational arrangements.

21. According to the above paragraph, an organization chart can be expected to portray the
    A. structure of the organization along somewhat ideal lines
    B. relative size of the organizational units quite accurately
    C. channels of information distribution within the organization graphically
    D. extent of the obligation of each unit to meet the organizational objectives

22. According to the above paragraph, those aspects of internal functioning which are NOT shown on an organization chart
    A. can be considered to have little practical application in the operations of the organization
    B. might well be considered to be as important as the structural relationships which a chart does present
    C. could be the cause of considerable confusion in the operation of an organization which is quite large
    D. would be most likely to provide the information needed to determine the overall effectiveness of an organization

23. In the above paragraph, the one of the following conditions which is NOT implied as being a defect of an organization chart is that an organization chart may
    A. present a picture of the organizational structure which is different from the structure that actually exists
    B. fail to indicate the comparative size of various organizational units
    C. be limited in its ability to convey some of the meaningful aspects of organizational relationships
    D. become less useful over a period of time during which the organizational facts which it illustrated have changed

24. The one of the following which is the MOST suitable title for the above paragraph is
    A. The Design and Construction of an Organization Chart
    B. The Informal Aspects of an Organization Chart
    C. The Inherent Deficiencies of an Organization Chart
    D. The Utilization of a Typical Organization Chart

25. It can be INFERRED from the above paragraph that the function of an organization chart is to
    A. contribute to the comprehension of the organization form and arrangements
    B. establish the capabilities of the organization to operate effectively
    C. provide a balanced picture of the operations of the organization
    D. eliminate the need for complexity in the organization's structure

KEY (CORRECT ANSWERS)

1. D
2. C
3. D
4. B
5. A

6. C
7. B
8. A
9. A
10. D

11. C
12. B
13. B
14. D
15. A

16. A
17. D
18. B
19. B
20. C

21. A
22. B
23. D
24. C
25. A

TEST 3

DIRECTIONS: Each question or incomplete statement is followed by several suggested answers or completions. Select the one that BEST answers the question or completes the statement. *PRINT THE LETTER OF THE CORRECT ANSWER IN THE SPACE AT THE RIGHT.*

1. Of the following problems that might affect the conduct and outcome of an interview, the MOST troublesome and usually the MOST difficult for the interviewer to control is the
   A. tendency of the interviewee to anticipate the needs and preferences of the interviewer
   B. impulse to cut the interviewee off when he seems to have reached the end of an idea
   C. tendency of interviewee attitudes to bias the results
   D. tendency of the interviewer to do most of the talking

2. The administrative assistant MOST likely to be a good interviewer is one who
   A. is adept at manipulating people and circumstances toward his objectives
   B. is able to put himself in the position of the interviewee
   C. gets the more difficult questions out of the way at the beginning of the interview
   D. develops one style and technique that can be used in any type of interview

3. A good interviewer guards against the tendency to form an overall opinion about an interviewee on the basis of a single aspect of the interviewee's make-up
   A. assumption error   B. expectancy error
   C. extension effect   D. halo effect

4. In conducting an exit interview with an employee who is leaving voluntarily, the interviewer's MAIN objective should be to
   A. see that the employee leaves with a good opinion of the organization
   B. learn the true reasons for the employee's resignation
   C. find out if the employee would consider a transfer
   D. try to get the employee to remain on the job

5. During an interview, an interviewee discloses a relevant but embarrassing personal fact.
   It would be BEST for the interviewer to
   A. listen calmly, avoiding any gesture or facial expression that would suggest approval or disapproval of what is related
   B. change the subject, since further discussion in this area may reveal other embarrassing, but irrelevant, personal facts
   C. apologize to the interviewee for having led him to reveal such a fact and promise not to do so again
   D. bring the interview to a close as quickly as possible in order to avoid a discussion which may be distressful to the interviewee

2 (#3)

6. Suppose that while you are interviewing an applicant for a position in your office, you notice a contradiction in facts in two of his responses.
   For you to call the contradictions to his attention would be
   A. *inadvisable*, because it reduces the interviewee's level of participation
   B. *advisable*, because getting the facts is essential to a successful interview
   C. *inadvisable*, because the interviewer should use more subtle techniques to resolve any discrepancies
   D. *advisable*, because the interviewee should be impressed with the necessity for giving consistent answers

   6._____

7. An interviewer should be aware that an undesirable result of including *leading questions* in an interview is to
   A. cause the interviewee to give *yes* or *no* answers with qualification or explanation
   B. encourage the interviewee to discuss irrelevant topics
   C. encourage the interviewee to give more meaningful information
   D. reduce the validity of the information obtained from the interviewee

   7._____

8. The kind of interview which is PARTICULARLY helpful in getting an employee to tell about his complaints and grievances is one in which
   A. a pattern has been worked out involving a sequence of exact questions to be asked
   B. the interviewee is expected to support his statements with specific evidence
   C. the interviewee is not made to answer specific questions but is encouraged to talk freely
   D. the interviewer has specific items on which he wishes to get or give information

   8._____

9. Suppose you are scheduled to interview a student aide under your supervision concerning a health problem. You know that some of the questions you will be asked him will seem embarrassing to him, and that he may resist answering these questions.
   In general, to hold these questions for the last part of the interview would be
   A. *desirable*; the intervening time period gives the interviewer an opportunity to plan how to ask these sensitive questions
   B. *undesirable*; the student aide will probably feel that he has been tricked when he suddenly must answer embarrassing questions
   C. *desirable*; the student aide will probably have increased confidence in the interviewer and be more willing to answer these questions
   D. *undesirable*; questions that are important should not be deferred until the end of the interview

   9._____

10. The House passed an amendment to delete from the omnibus higher education bill a section that would have prohibited coeducational colleges and universities from considering sex as a factor in their admissions policy.
    According to the above passage, consideration of sex as a factor in the admissions policy of coeducational colleges and universities would

    10._____

A. be permitted by the omnibus higher education bill if passed without further amendment
B. be prohibited by the amendment to the omnibus higher education bill
C. have been prohibited by the deletion of a section from the omnibus higher education bill
D. have been permitted if the house had failed to pass the amendment

Questions 11-14.

DIRECTIONS: Questions 11 through 14 are to be answered SOLELY according to the information given in the following passage.

The proposition that administrative activity is essentially the same in all organizations appears to underlie some of the practices in the administration of private higher education. Although the practice is unusual in public education, there are numerous instances of industrial, governmental, or military administrators being assigned to private institutions of higher education and, to a lesser extent, of college and university presidents assuming administrative positions in other types of organizations. To test this theory that administrators are interchangeable, there is a need for systematic observation and classification. The myth that an educational administrator must first have experience in the teaching profession is firmly rooted in a long tradition that has historical prestige. The myth is bound up in the expectations of the public and personnel surrounding the administrator. Since administrative success depends significantly on how well an administrator meets the expectations others have of him, the myth may be more powerful than the special experience in helping the administrator attain organizational and educational objectives. Educational administrators who have risen through the teaching profession have often expressed nostalgia for the life of a teacher or scholar, but there is no evidence that this nostalgia contributes to administrative success.

11. Which of the following statements as completed is MOST consistent with the above passage?
The greatest number of administrators has moved from
    A. industry and the military to government and universities
    B. government and universities to industry and the military
    C. government, the armed forces, and industry to colleges and universities
    D. colleges and universities to government, the armed forces, and industry

11._____

12. Of the following, the MOST reasonable inference from the above passage is that a specific area requiring research is the
    A. place of myth in the tradition and history of the educational profession
    B. relative effectiveness of educational administrators from inside and outside the teaching profession
    C. performance of administrators in the administration of public colleges
    D. degree of reality behind the nostalgia for scholarly pursuits often expressed by educational administrators

12._____

13. According to the above passage, the value to an educational administrator of experience in the teaching profession
    A. lies in the first-hand knowledge he has acquired of immediate educational problems
    B. may lie in the belief of his colleagues, subordinates, and the public that such experience is necessary
    C. has been supported by evidence that the experience contributes to administrative success in educational fields
    D. would be greater if the administrator were able to free himself from nostalgia for his former duties

13.____

14. Of the following, the MOST appropriate title for the above passage is
    A. Educational Administration, Its problems
    B. The Experience Needed for Educational Administration
    C. Administration in Higher Education
    D. Evaluating Administrative Experience

14.____

Questions 15-20.

DIRECTIONS: Questions 15 through 20 are to be answered SOLELY according to the information contained in the following paragraph.

Methods of administration of office activities, much of which consists of providing information and "know-how" needed to coordinate both activities within that particular office and other offices, have been among the last to come under the spotlight of management analysis. Progress has been rapid during the past decade, however, and is now accelerating at such a pace that an "information revolution" in office management appears to be in the making. Although triggered by technological breakthroughs in electronic computers and other giant steps in mechanization, this information revolution must be attributed to underlying forces, such as the increased complexity of both governmental and private enterprise, and ever-keener competition. Size, diversification, specialization of function, and decentralization are among the forces which make coordination of activities both more imperative and more difficult. Increased competition, both domestic and international, leaves little margin for error in managerial decisions. Several developments during recent years indicate an evolving pattern. In 1960, the American Management Association expanded the scope of its activities and changed the name of its Office Management Division to Administrative Service Division. Also in 1960, the magazine Office Management merged with the magazine American Business, and this new publication was named Administrative Management.

15. A REASONABLE inference that can be made from the information in the above paragraph is that an important role of the office manager today is to
    A. work toward specialization of functions performed by his subordinates
    B. inform and train subordinates regarding any new developments in computer technology and mechanization
    C. assist the professional management analysts with the management analysis work in the organization
    D. supply information that can be used to help coordinate and manager the other activities of the organization

15.____

16. An IMPORTANT reason for the "information revolution" that has been taking place in office management is the
    A. advance made in management analysis in the past decade
    B. technological breakthrough in electronic computers and mechanization
    C. more competitive and complicated nature of private business and government
    D. increased efficiency of office management techniques in the past ten years

17. According to the above paragraph, specialization of function in an organization is MOST likely to result in
    A. the elimination of errors in managerial decisions
    B. greater need to coordinate activities
    C. more competition with other organizations, both domestic and international
    D. a need for office managers with greater flexibility

18. The word *evolving*, as used in the third from last sentence in the above paragraph, means MOST NEARLY
    A. developing by gradual changes
    B. passing on to others
    C. occurring periodically
    D. breaking up into separate, constituent parts

19. Of the following, the MOST reasonable implication of the changes in names mentioned in the last part of the above paragraph is that these groups are attempting to
    A. professionalize the field of office management and the title of Office Manager
    B. combine two publications into one because of the increased costs of labor and materials
    C. adjust to the fact that the field of office management is broadening
    D. appeal to the top managerial people rather than the office management people in business and government

20. According to the above paragraph, intense competition among domestic and international enterprises makes it MOST important for an organization's managerial staff to
    A. coordinate and administer office activities with other activities in the organization
    B. make as few errors in decision-making as possible
    C. concentrate on decentralization and reduction of size of the individual divisions of the organization
    D. restrict decision-making only to top management officials

KEY (CORRECT ANSWERS)

1.	A	11.	C
2.	B	12.	B
3.	D	13.	B
4.	B	14.	B
5.	A	15.	D
6.	B	16.	C
7.	D	17.	B
8.	C	18.	A
9.	C	19.	C
10.	A	20.	B

EXAMINATION SECTION
TEST 1

DIRECTIONS: Each question or incomplete statement is followed by several suggested answers or completions. Select the one that BEST answers the question or completes the statement. *PRINT THE LETTER OF THE CORRECT ANSWER IN THE SPACE AT THE RIGHT.*

1. In discussing with a subordinate the assignment which you are giving him, it is MOST important that you place greatest stress on
    A. the immediate job to be done
    B. what was accomplished in the past
    C. the long-term goals of the organization
    D. what others have accomplished

2. Personal friendship and intimacy exhibited by the administrative assistant toward his subordinates should ALWAYS be
    A. kept to a bare minimum
    B. free and unrestricted
    C. in accordance with the personal qualities of each individual subordinate
    D. tempered by the need for objectivity

3. Assume that one of the office assistants under your supervision approaches you and asks if would give her advice on some problems that she is having with her husband.
   Of the following, the MOST appropriate action for you to take is to
    A. tell her that she would be making a mistake in discussing it with you
    B. listen briefly to her problem and then suggest how she might get help in solving it
    C. give her whatever advice she needs based on your knowledge or experience in this area
    D. refer her to a lawyer specializing in marital problems

4. When you return from lunch one day, you find Miss P, one of your subordinates, in your office crying uncontrollably. When she calms down, she tells you that Mr. T, another subordinate, insulted her but she would prefer not to give details because they are very personal.
   Your IMMEDIATE reaction should be to
    A. reprimand Mr. T for his callousness
    B. reprimand the worker in your office for not controlling herself
    C. get as much information as possible about exactly what happened
    D. tell Miss P that she will have to take care of her own affairs

5. If one of the office assistants under your supervision does not seem to be able to get along well with the other employees, the FIRST step that you should take in such a situation should be to try to find out
   A. more about the background of the office assistant
   B. the reason the office assistant has difficulty in getting along
   C. if another department would be interested in employing the office assistant
   D. the procedures required for dismissal of the office assistant

6. Suppose that you expect that your department will send two of your subordinates for outside training on the use of new office equipment while others will be trained on the job.
   When preparing a yearly budget and schedule for the personnel that you supervise, training costs to be paid for by the department should be
   A. excluded and treated separately as a special request when the specific training need arises
   B. estimated and included in the budget and manpower schedules
   C. left out of the schedule since personnel are thoroughly trained before assignment to a position
   D. considered only if training involves time away from the job

7. There is a rumor going around your department that one of the administrative assistants is going to resign.
   Since it is not true, the BEST action to take would be to
   A. find the person starting the rumor and advise him that disciplinary action will follow if the rumors do not stop
   B. disregard the rumor since the grapevine is always inaccurate
   C. tell the truth about the situation to those concerned
   D. start another rumor yourself that contradicts this rumor

8. Suppose a student is concerned over the possibility of failing a course and losing matriculated status. He comes to you for advice.
   The BEST thing for you to do is to
   A. tell the student it is not your function to discuss student problems
   B. impress the student with the importance of academic performance and suggest that more study is necessary
   C. send the student to a career counselor for testing
   D. suggest that he see the instructor or appropriate faculty advisor depending on the cause of the problem

9. A member of the faculty had requested that an overhead projector be reserved for a seminar. At the time of the seminar, the projector has not been placed in the room, and you find that one of your office assistants forgot to send the request to the building staff.
   Of the following possible actions, which one should be taken FIRST?
   A. See to it that the projector is moved to the seminar room immediately
   B. Personally reprimand the subordinate responsible

C. Suggest rescheduling the seminar
D. Tell the faculty member that the problem was caused by a fault in the machine

10. Assume that you have to give work assignments to a male office assistant and a female office assistant.
    It would be BEST to
    A. allow the woman to have first choice of assignments
    B. give the female preference in assignments requiring patience
    C. give the male preference in assignments requiring physical action
    D. make assignments to each on the basis of demonstrated ability and interest

11. In the initial phase of training a new employee to perform his job, which of the following approaches is MOST desirable?
    A. Have him read the office manual
    B. Tell him to watch the other employees
    C. Give him simple tasks to perform
    D. Have him do exactly what everyone else is doing

12. Assume that one of the employees under your supervision performs her work adequately, but you feel that she might be more productive if she changed some of her methods.
    You should
    A. discuss with her those changes which you think would be helpful
    B. refrain from saying anything since her work is adequate
    C. suggest that she might be helped by talking to a guidance counselor
    D. assign her to another job

13. One of the office assistants under your supervision complains to you that the report which you assigned her to prepare is monotonous work and unnecessary. The report is a monthly compilation of figures which you submit to your superior.
    Of the following, the BEST action to take FIRST is to
    A. ask her why she feels the work is unnecessary
    B. tell her that she is employed to do whatever work is assigned to her
    C. have her do other work at the same time to provide more interest
    D. assign the report to another subordinate

14. Of the following, the GREATEST advantage of keeping records of the quantity of work produced by the office assistants under your supervision is to
    A. have the statistics available in case they are required
    B. enable you to take appropriate action in case of increase, decrease, or other variation in output
    C. provide a basis for promotion or other personnel action
    D. give you a basis for requesting additional employees

15. It is not possible to achieve maximum productivity from your subordinates *unless* they are told 15.____
    A. what the rewards are for their performance
    B. how they will be punished for failure
    C. what it is they are expected to do
    D. that they must work hard if they are to succeed

16. Suppose that you observe that one of the assistants on your staff is involved with an extremely belligerent student who is demanding information that is not readily available in your department. One staff member is becoming visibly upset and is apparently about to lose his temper. 16.____
    Under these circumstances, it would be BEST for you to
    A. leave the room and let the situation work itself out
    B. let the assistant lose his temper, then intervene and calm both parties at the same time
    C. step in immediately and try to calm the student in order to suggest more expedient ways of getting the information
    D. tell the student to come back and discuss the situation when he can do it calmly

17. Suppose you have explained an assignment to a newly appointed clerk and the clerk has demonstrated her ability to do the work. After a short period of time, the clerk tells you that she is afraid of incorrectly completing the assignment. 17.____
    Of the following, the BEST course of action for you to take is to
    A. tell her to observe another clerk who is doing the same type of work
    B. explain to her the importance of the assignment and tell her not to be nervous
    C. assign her another task which is easier to perform
    D. try to allay her fears and encourage her to try to do the work

Questions 18-22.

DIRECTIONS: Questions 18 through 22 consist of the names of students who have applied for a certain college program and are to be classified according to the criteria described below.

The following table gives pertinent data for 6 different applicants with regard to:
Grade averages, which are expressed on a scale running from 0 (low) to 4 (high);
Scores on qualifying test, which run from 200 (low) to 800 (high);
Related work experience, which is expressed in number of months;
Personal references, which are rated from 1 (low) to 5 (high).

Applicant	Grade Average	Test Score	Work Experience	Reference
Jones	2.2	620	24	3
Perez	3.5	650	0	5
Lowitz	3.2	420	2	4
Uncker	2.1	710	15	2
Farrow	2.8	560	0	3
Shapiro	3.0	560	12	4

An administrative assistant is in charge of the initial screening process for the program. This process requires classifying applicants into the following four groups:

- A. SUPERIOR CANDIDATES: Unless the personal reference rating is lower than 3, all applicants with grade averages of 3.0 or higher and test scores of 600 or higher are classified as superior candidates.
- B. GOOD CANDIDATES: Unless the personal reference rating is lower than 3, all applicants with one of the following combinations of grade averages and test scores are classified as good candidates: (1) grade average of 2.5 to 2.9 and test score of 600 or higher; (2) grade average of 3.0 or higher and test score of 550 to 599.
- C. POSSIBLE CANDIDATES: Applicants with one of the following combinations of qualifications are classified as possible candidates: (1) grade average of 2.5 to 2.9 and test score of 550 to 599 and a personal reference rating of 3 or higher; (2) grade average of 2.0 to 2.4 and test score of 500 or higher and at least 21 months' work experience and a personal reference rating of 3 or higher; (3) a combination of grade average and test score that would otherwise qualify as *superior* or *good* but a personal reference score lower than 3.
- D. REJECTED CANDIDATES: Applicants who do not fall in any of the above groups are to be rejected.

EXAMPLE

Jones' grade average of 2.2 does not meet the standard for either a superior candidate (grade average must be 3.0 or higher) or a good candidate (grade average must be 2.5 to 2.9). Grade average of 2.2 does not qualify Jones as a possible candidate if Jones has a test score of 500 or higher, at least 21 months' work experience, and a personal reference rating of 3 or higher. Since Jones has a test score of 620, 24 months' work experience, and a reference rating of 3, Jones is a possible candidate. The answer is C.

Answer Questions 18 through 22 as explained above, indicating for each whether the applicant should be classified as a
- A. superior candidate
- B. good candidate
- C. possible candidate
- D. rejected candidate

18. Perez

19. Lowitz

20. Uncker

21. Farrow   21._____

22. Shapiro   22._____

23. A new training program is being set up for which certain new forms will be   23._____
    needed. You have been asked to design these forms.
    Of the following, the FIRST step you should take in planning the forms is
    A. finding out the exact purpose for which each form will be used
    B. deciding what size of paper should be used for each form
    C. determining whether multiple copies will be needed for any of the forms
    D. setting up a new filing system to handle the new forms

24. You have been asked to write a report on methods of hiring and training new   24._____
    employees. Your report is going to be about ten pages long.
    For the convenience of your readers, a brief summary of your findings should
    A. appear at the beginning of your report
    B. be appended to the report as a postscript
    C. be circulated in a separate memo
    D. be inserted in tabular form in the middle of your report

25. Assume that your department is being moved to new and larger quarters, and   25._____
    that you have been asked to suggest an office layout for the central clerical
    office.
    Of the following, your FIRST step in planning the new layout should ordinarily
    be to
    A. find out how much money has been budgeted for furniture and equipment
    B. make out work-flow and traffic-flow charts for the clerical operations
    C. measure each piece of furniture and equipment that is presently in use
    D. determine which files should be moved to a storage area or destroyed

KEY (CORRECT ANSWERS)

1. A
2. D
3. B
4. C
5. B

6. B
7. C
8. D
9. A
10. D

11. C
12. A
13. A
14. B
15. C

16. C
17. D
18. A
19. D
20. D

21. C
22. B
23. A
24. A
25. B

TEST 2

DIRECTIONS: Each question or incomplete statement is followed by several suggested answers or completions. Select the one that BEST answers the question or completes the statement. *PRINT THE LETTER OF THE CORRECT ANSWER IN THE SPACE AT THE RIGHT.*

1. In modern office layouts, screens and dividers are often used instead of walls to set off working groups.
   Advantages given for this approach have included all of the following EXCEPT
   - A. more frequent communication between different working groups
   - B. reduction in general noise level
   - C. fewer objections from employees who are transferred to different groups
   - D. cost savings from increased sharing of office equipment

   1._____

2. Of the following, the CHIEF reason for moving less active material from active to inactive files is to
   - A. dispose of material that no longer has any use
   - B. keep the active files down to a manageable size
   - C. make sure that no material over a year old remains in active files
   - D. separate temporary records from permanent records

   2._____

3. The use of a microfiche system for information storage and retrieval would make MOST sense in an office where
   - A. a great number of documents must be kept available for permanent reference
   - B. documents are ordinarily kept on file for less than six months
   - C. filing is a minor and unimportant part of office work
   - D. most of the records on file are working forms on which additional entries are frequently made

   3._____

4. The work loads in different offices fluctuate greatly over the course of a year. Ordinarily, the MOST economical way of handling a peak load in a specific office is to
   - A. hire temporary help from an outside agency
   - B. require regular employees to put in overtime
   - C. use employees from other offices that are not busy
   - D. buy special equipment for operations that can be automated

   4._____

5. A faculty member has given you a long list of student grades to be typed. Since your typed list will be the basis for permanent records, it is essential that it contain no errors.
   The BEST way of checking this typed list is to
   - A. ask the faculty member to glance over the typed version and have him correct any mistakes
   - B. have someone read the handwritten list aloud, while you check the typed list as each item is read

   5._____

28

C. read the typed list yourself to see that it makes good sense and that there are no omissions or duplications
D. make a spot-check by comparing several entries in the typed list against the original entries on the handwritten list

6. It is necessary to purchase a machine for your department which will be used to make single copies of documents and to make copies of memos that are distributed to as many as 150 people.
Of the following kinds of machines, which one is BEST suited for your department's purposes?
A(n)
 A. laser copier
 B. fax machine
 C. inkjet printer
 D. multipage scanner

6._____

7. Suppose that faculty members have fallen into the habit of asking clerical employees in your department to perform messenger service between your building and other parts of the school. Such demands are becoming increasingly common, and you feel that the two or three man-hours per day involved is too much. Furthermore, these assignments disrupt the work of the department.
Of the following solutions, which one is MOST likely to result in the GREATEST efficiency?
 A. Hire a full-time messenger whose only job will be to run intra-school errands
 B. Establish a rule that no employees in your department will act as messengers under any circumstances, and that all materials must be sent by ordinary interoffice mail
 C. Notify other departments that from now on they must use their own employees for messenger service to or from your building
 D. Allow the clerical employees to perform messenger service only in cases of urgent need, and have interoffice mail used in all other cases

7._____

8. A new employee is trying to file records for three different students whose names are Robinson, John L., Robinson, John, and Robinson, John Leonard. The employee does not know in what order the records should be filed.
You should
 A. tell the employee to use whatever order seems most convenient
 B. suggest that all the records be put in one folder and arranged chronologically according to date of enrollment
 C. explain that, by the *nothing-before-something* principle, John comes first, John L. second, and John Leonard last
 D. instruct the employee to keep them together but arrange them chronologically according to date of birth

8._____

9. An *out card* or *out guide* should be placed in a file drawer to mark the location of material that
   A. has not yet been received
   B. should be transferred to an inactive file
   C. has been temporarily removed
   D. is no longer needed

10. Assume that your office does not presently have a formal records-retention program. Your supervisor has suggested that such a program be set up, and has asked you go make a study and submit your recommendations.
    The FIRST step in your study should be to
    A. find out how long it has been since the files were last cleaned out
    B. take an inventory of the types of materials now in the files
    C. learn how much storage space you can obtain for old records
    D. decide which files should be thrown out instead of being stored

11. In an organization where a great deal of time and money is spent on information management, it often makes sense to use a *systems analysis* approach in reviewing operations and deciding how they can be carried out more efficiently.
    Of the following, the FIRST question that a *systems analysis* should ask about any procedure
    A. whether the procedure can be handled by automatic data-processing equipment
    B. exactly how the procedure is meshed with other existing procedures used in the organization
    C. how many employees should be hired to carry out the present procedure
    D. what is the end result that the use of the procedure is supposed to achieve

12. You have been notified that a *work simplification* study is going to be carried out in your department.
    The one of the following which is MOST likely to be the purpose of this study is to
    A. increase the productivity of the office by eliminating unnecessary procedures and irrelevant record keeping
    B. produce a new office manual that explains current procedures in a simple and easily understandable way
    C. determine whether there are any procedures so simple that they can be handled by untrained workers
    D. substitute computer processing for all operations that are now performed manually

13. Suppose that a cost study has been made of various clerical procedures carried out in your college, and that the study shows that the average cost of a dictated business letter is over $5.00 per letter.
    Of the following cost factors that go into making up this total cost, the LARGEST single factor is certain to be the cost of
    A. stationery and postage   B. office machinery
    C. labor   D. office rental

14. Which of the following software programs is BEST for collecting and sorting data, creating graphs, and preparing spreadsheets?
    A. Microsoft Excel
    B. Microsoft Word
    C. Microsoft Powerpoint
    D. QuarkXPress

15. Which of the following software programs is BEST for creating visual presentations containing text, photos, and charts?
    A. Microsoft Excel
    B. Microsoft Outlook
    C. Microsoft Powerpoint
    D. Adobe Photoshop

16. A supervisor asks you to e-mail a file that has been saved on your computer as a photograph. Since you do not remember the file name, you must search by file type.
    Which of the following file extensions should you run a search for?
    A. .html
    B. .pdf
    C. .jpg
    D. .doc

17. In records management, the term *vital records* refers generally to papers that
    A. are essential to life
    B. are needed for an office to continue operating after fire or other disaster
    C. contain statistics about birth and death
    D. can be easily replaced

18. A city agency maintains a complete set of records on its clients on a central computer. A branch office finds that it frequently needs access to this data. A computer output device which could be installed in the branch office to provide the data is called a
    A. sorter
    B. tabulator
    C. card punch
    D. terminal

19. A certain employee is paid at the rate of $18.20 per hour, with time-and-a-half for overtime. Hours in excess of 40 hours a week count as overtime. During the past week, the employee put in 44 working hours.
    The employee's gross wages for the week are MOST NEARLY
    A. $736
    B. $792
    C. $828
    D. $888

20. You are making a report on the number of inside and outside calls handled by a particular switchboard. Over a 5-day period, the total number of all inside and outside calls handled by the switchboard was 2,314. The average number of inside calls per day was 274. You cannot find one day's tally of outside calls, but the total number of outside calls for the other four days was 776. From this information, how many outside calls must have been reported on the missing tally?
    A. 168
    B. 190
    C. 194
    D. 274

21. One typist can type 100 address labels in 1 hour. Another typist can type 100 address labels in 1 hour and 15 minutes.
    If there are 450 address labels to be typed and both typists are put to work on the job, how soon can they be expected to finish the work?
    In _____ hours.
    A. 2¼
    B. 2½
    C. 4½
    D. 5

22. A floor plan has been prepared for a new building, drawn to a scale of ½ inch = 1 foot. A certain area is drawn 1 foot long and 7½ inches wide on the floor plan.
    The actual dimensions of this area in the new building are _____ feet long and _____ feet wide.
    A. 6; 3¼   B. 12; 7½   C. 20; 15   D. 24; 15

23. In recent years a certain college has admitted a number of students with high school grades of C-plus or lower. It has usually turned out that an average of 65% of these students completed their freshman year. Last year 340 such students were admitted. By the end of the year, 102 of these students were no longer in college, but the others completed successfully.
    How many MORE students completed the year than would have been expected, based on the average results of previous years?
    A. 14   B. 17   C. 39   D. 119

24. The morale of employees is an important factor in the maintenance of job interest.
    Which of the following is generally LEAST valuable in strengthening morale?
    A. Attempting to take a personal interest in one's subordinates
    B. Encouraging employees to speak openly about their opinions and suggestions
    C. Fostering a feeling of group spirit among the workers
    D. Having all employees work at the same rate

25. Of the following, the BEST way for a supervisor to determine when *further* on-the-job training in a particular work area is needed is by
    A. asking the employees
    B. evaluating the employees' work performance
    C. determining the ratio of idle time to total work time
    D. classifying the jobs in the work area

KEY (CORRECT ANSWERS)

1. B
2. B
3. A
4. C
5. B

6. A
7. D
8. C
9. C
10. B

11. D
12. A
13. C
14. A
15. C

16. C
17. B
18. D
19. C
20. A

21. B
22. D
23. B
24. D
25. B

EXAMINATION SECTION
TEST 1

DIRECTIONS: Each question or incomplete statement is followed by several suggested answers or completions. Select the one that BEST answers the question or completes the statement. *PRINT THE LETTER OF THE CORRECT ANSWER IN THE SPACE AT THE RIGHT.*

Questions 1-6.

DIRECTIONS: Questions 1 through 6 each consist of four sentences. Choose the one sentence in each set of four that would be BEST for a formal letter or report. Consider grammar and appropriate usage.

1. A. These statements can be depended upon, for their truth has been guaranteed by reliable city employees.
    B. Reliable city employees guarantee the facts with regards to the truth of these statements.
    C. Most all these statements have been supported by city employees who are reliable and can be depended upon.
    D. The city employees which have guaranteed these statements are reliable.

    1.____

2. A. I believe the letter was addressed to either my associate or I.
    B. If properly addressed, the letter will reach my associate and I.
    C. My associate's name, as well as mine, was on the letter.
    D. The letter had been addressed to myself and my associate.

    2.____

3. A. The secretary would have corrected the errors if she knew that the supervisor would see the report.
    B. The supervisor reprimanded the secretary, whom she believed had made careless errors.
    C. Many errors were found in the report which she typed and could not disregard them.
    D. The errors in the typed report were so numerous that they could hardly be overlooked.

    3.____

4. A. His consultant was as pleased as he with the success of the project.
    B. The success of the project pleased both his consultant and he.
    C. he and also his consultant was pleased with the success of the project.
    D. Both his consultant and he was pleased with the success of the project.

    4.____

5. A. Since the letter did not contain the needed information, it was not real useful to him.
    B. Being that the letter lacked the needed information, he could not use it.
    C. Since the letter lacked the needed information, it was of no use to him.
    D. This letter was useless to him because there was no needed information in it.

    5.____

6. A. Scarcely had the real estate tax increase been declared than the notices were sent out.
    B. They had no sooner declared the real estate tax increases when they sent the notices to the owners.
    C. The city had hardly declared the real estate tax increase till the notices were prepared for mailing.
    D. No sooner had the real estate tax been declared than the notices were sent out.

Questions 7-14.

DIRECTIONS: Questions 7 through 14 are to be answered on the basis of the following passage.

Important figures in education and in public affairs have recommended development of a private organization sponsored in part by various private foundations which would offer installment payment plans to full-time matriculated students in accredited colleges and universities in the United States and Canada. Contracts would be drawn to cover either tuition and fees, or tuition, fees, room and board in college facilities, from one year up to and including six years. A special charge, which would vary with the length of the contract, would be added to the gross repayable amount. This would be in addition to interest at a rate which would vary with the income of the parents. There would be a 3% annual interest charge for families with total income, before income taxes of $10,000 or less. The rate would increase by 1/10 of 1% for every $200 of additional net income in excess of $10,000 up to a maximum of 10% interest. Contracts would carry an insurance provision on the life of the parent or guardian who signs the contract; all contracts must have the signature of a parent or guardian. Payment would be scheduled in equal monthly installments.

7. Which of the following students would be eligible for the payment plan described in the above passage? A
    A. matriculated student taking 6 semester hours toward a graduate degree at CCNY
    B. matriculated student taking 17 semester hours toward an undergraduate degree at Brooklyn College
    C. CCNY graduate matriculated at the University of Mexico, taking 18 semester hours toward a graduate degree
    D. student taking 18 semester hours in a special pre-matriculation program at Hunter College

8. According to the above passage, the organization described would be sponsored in part by
    A. private foundations
    B. colleges and universities
    C. persons in the field of education
    D. persons in public life

9. Which of the following expenses could NOT be covered by a contract with the organization described in the above passage?
   A. Tuition amounting to $4,000 per year
   B. Registration and laboratory fees
   C. Meals at restaurants near the college
   D. Rent for an apartment in a college dormitory

10. The total amount to be paid would include ONLY the
    A. principal
    B. principal and interest
    C. principal, interest, and special charge
    D. principal, interest, special charge, and fee

11. The contract would carry insurance on the
    A. life of the student
    B. life of the student's parents
    C. income of the parents of the student
    D. life of the parent who signed the contract

12. The interest rate for an annual loan of $5,000 from the organization described in the passage for a student whose family's net income was $11,000 should be
    A. 3%   B. 3.5%   C. 4%   D. 4.5%

13. The interest rate for an annual loan of $7,000 from the organization described in the passage for a student whose family's net income was $20,000 should be
    A. 5%   B. 8%   C. 9%   D. 10%

14. John Lee has submitted an application for the installment payment plan described in the passage. John's mother and father have a store which grossed $100,000 last year, but the income which the family received from the store was $18,000 before taxes. They also had $1,000 income from stock dividends. They paid $2,000 in income taxes.
    The amount of income upon which the interest should be based is
    A. $17,000   B. $18,000   C. $19,000   D. $21,000

15. One of the MOST important techniques for conducting good interviews is
    A. asking the applicant questions in rapid succession, thereby keeping the conversation properly focused
    B. listening carefully to all that the applicant has to say, making mental notes of possible areas for follow-up
    C. indicating to the applicant the criteria and standards on which you will base your judgment
    D. making sure that you are interrupted above five minutes before you wish to end so that you can keep on schedue

16. You are planning to conduct preliminary interviews of applicants for an important position in your department.
    Which of the following planning considerations is LEAST likely to contribute to successful interviews?
    A. Make provisions to conduct interviews in privacy
    B. Schedule your appointments so that interviews will be short
    C. Prepare a list of your objectives
    D. Learn as much as you can about the applicant before the interview

17. In interviewing job applicants, which of the following usually does NOT have to be done before the end of the interview?
    A. Making a decision to hire an applicant
    B. Securing information from applicants
    C. Giving information to applicants
    D. Establishing a friendly relationship with applicants

18. In the process of interviewing applicants for a position on your staff, the one of the following which would be BEST is to
    A. make sure all applicants are introduced to the other members of your staff prior to the formal interview
    B. make sure the applicant does not ask questions about the job or the department
    C. avoid having the applicant talk with the staff under any circumstances
    D. introduce applicants to some of the staff at the conclusion of a successful interview

19. While interviewing a job applicant, you ask why the applicant left his last job. The applicant does not answer immediately.
    Of the following, the BEST action to take at that point is to
    A. wait until he answers
    B. ask another question
    C. repeat the question in a loud voice
    D. ask him why he does not answer

20. Which of the following actions would be LEAST desirable for you to take when you have to conduct an interview?
    A. Set a relaxed and friendly atmosphere
    B. Plan your interview ahead of time
    C. Allow the person interviewed to structure the interview as he wishes
    D. Include some stock or standard question which you ask everyone

21. You know that a student applying for a job in your office has done well in college except for two courses in science. However, when you ask him about his grades, his reply is vague and general.
    It would be BEST for you to
    A. lead the applicant to admitting doing poorly in science to be sure that the facts are correct
    B. judge the applicant's tact and skill in handling what may be for him a personally sensitive question

C. immediately confront the applicant with the facts and ask for an explanation
D. ignore the applicant's response since you have the transcript

22. A college student has applied for a position with your department. Prior to conducting an interview of the job applicant, it would be LEAST helpful for you to have
    A. a personal resume
    B. a job description
    C. references
    D. hiring requirements

    22.____

23. Job applicants tend to be nervous during interviews.
    Which of the following techniques is MOST likely to put such an applicant at ease?
    A. Try to establish rapport by asking general questions which are easily answered by the applicant
    B. Ask the applicant to describe his career objectives immediately, thus minimizing the anxiety caused by waiting
    C. Start the interview with another member of the staff present so that the applicant does not feel alone
    D. Proceed as rapidly as possible, since the emotional state of the applicant is none of your concern

    23.____

24. Of the following abilities, the one which is LEAST important in conducting an interview is the ability to
    A. ask the interviewee pertinent questions
    B. evaluate the interviewee on the basis of appearance
    C. evaluate the responses of the interviewee
    D. gain the cooperation of the interviewee

    24.____

25. One of the techniques of management often used by supervisors is performance appraisal.
    Which of the following is NOT one of the objectives of performance appraisal?
    A. Improve staff performance
    B. Determine individual training needs
    C. Improve organizational structure
    D. Set standards and performance criteria for employees

    25.____

KEY (CORRECT ANSWERS)

1.	A	11.	D
2.	C	12.	B
3.	D	13.	B
4.	A	14.	C
5.	C	15.	B
6.	D	16.	B
7.	B	17.	A
8.	A	18.	D
9.	C	19.	A
10.	C	20.	C

21. B
22. C
23. A
24. B
25. C

TEST 2

DIRECTIONS: Each question or incomplete statement is followed by several suggested answers or completions. Select the one that BEST answers the question or completes the statement. *PRINT THE LETTER OF THE CORRECT ANSWER IN THE SPACE AT THE RIGHT.*

1. Examine the following sentence, and then choose the BEST statement about it from the choices below.
Clerks are expected to receive visitors, to answer telephones, and miscellaneous clerical work must be done.
    A. This sentence is an example of effective writing.
    B. This is a run-on sentence.
    C. The three ideas in this sentence are not parallel, and therefore they should be divided into separate sentences.
    D. The three ideas in this sentence are parallel, but they are not expressed in parallel form.

1._____

2. Examine the following sentence, and then choose from below the word which should be inserted in the blank space.
Mr. Luce is a top-notch interviewer, _____ he is very reliable.
    A. but   B. and   C. however   D. for

2._____

3. Examine the following sentence, and then choose from below the words which should be inserted in the blank spaces.
The committee _____ sent in _____ report.
    A. has; it's   B. has; their   C. have; its   D. has; its

3._____

4. Examine the following sentence, and then choose from below the words which should be inserted in the blank spaces.
An organization usually contains more than just a few people; usually the membership is _____ enough so that close personal relationships among _____ impossible.
    A. large; are
    C. small; becomes
    B. large; found
    D. small; is

4._____

5. Of the following, the BEST reference book to use to find a synonym for a common word is a(n)
    A. thesaurus
    C. encyclopedia
    B. dictionary
    catalog

5._____

Questions 6-10.

DIRECTIONS: Questions 6 through 10 concern college students who have just completed their junior year for whom you must calculate grade averages for the year. These averages are to be based on the following table showing the number of credit hours for each student during the year at each of the grade levels: A, B, C, D, and F. How these letter grades may be translated into numerical grades is indicated in the first column of the table.

| Grade | Credit Hours – Junior Year | | | | | |
Value	King	Lewis	Martin	Nonkin	Ottly	Perry
A = 95	12	6	15	3	9	–
B = 85	9	15	6	12	9	3
C = 75	6	9	9	12	3	27
D = 65	3	–	3	3	6	–
F = 0	–	–	–	3	–	–

Calculating a grade average for an individual student is a 4-step process:
I. Multiply each grade value by the number of credit hours for which the student received that grade.
II. Add these multiplication products for each student.
III. Add the student's total credit hours.
IV. Divide the multiplication product total by the total number of credit hours.
V. Round the result, if there is a decimal place, to the nearest whole number. A number ending in .5 would be rounded to the next higher number.

EXAMPLE

Using student King's grades as an example, his grade average can be calculated by going through the following four steps.

I. 95 x 12 = 1140
   85 x 9 = 765
   75 x 6 = 450
   65 x 3 = 195
   65 x 3 =   0

II. Total   2550

III. 12
     9
     6
     2
     0
     30 Total Credit Hours

IV. Divide 2550 by 30: $\frac{2550}{30} = 85$

King's grade average is 85.

Questions 6 through 10 are to be answered on the basis of the information given above.

6. The grade average of Lewis is
   A. 83   B. 84   C. 85   D. 86

7. The grade average of Martin is
   A. 83   B. 84   C. 85   D. 86

8. The grade average of Nonkin is
   A. 72   B. 73   C. 79   D. 80

9. Student Ottly must attain a grade average of 85 in each of his years in college to be accepted into graduate school.
If, in summer school during his junior year, he takes two 3-credit courses and receives a grade of 85 in one and 95 in the other, his grade average for his junior year will then be MOST NEARLY
   A. 82   B. 83   C. 84   D. 85

10. If Perry takes an additional 3-credit course during the year and receives a grade of 95. his grade average will be increased to approximately
    A. 74   B. 76   C. 78   D. 80

11. You are in charge of verifying employees' qualifications. This involves telephoning previous employers and schools. One of the applications which you are reviewing contains information which you are almost certain is correct on the basis of what the employee has told you.
The BEST thing to do is to
    A. check the information again with the employee
    B. perform the required verification procedures
    C. accept the information as valid
    D. ask a superior to verify the information

12. The practice of immediately identifying oneself and one's place of employment when contacting persons on the telephone is
    A. *good*, because the receiver of the call can quickly identify the caller and establish a frame of reference
    B. *good*, because it helps to set the caller at ease with the other party
    C. *poor*, because it is not necessary to divulge that information when making general calls
    D. *poor*, because it takes longer to arrive at the topic to be discussed

13. A supervisor, Miss Smith, meets with a group of subordinates and tells them how they should perform certain tasks. The meeting is highly successful. She then attends a meeting to discuss common problems with a group of fellow supervisors with duties similar to her own. When she tells them how their subordinates should perform the same tasks, some of the other supervisors become angry.
Of the following, the MOST likely reason for this anger is that
    A. tension is to be expected in situations in which supervisors deal with each other
    B. the other supervisors are jealous of Miss Smith's knowledge
    C. Miss Smith should not tell other supervisors what methods she uses
    D. Miss Smith does not correctly perceive her role in relation to other supervisors

14. There is considerable rivalry among employees in a certain department over location of desks. It is the practice of the supervisor to assign desks without any predetermined plan. The supervisor is reconsidering his procedure.

In assigning desks, PRIMARY consideration should ordinarily be given to
A. past practices
B. flow of work
C. employee seniority
D. social relations among employees

15. Assume that, when you tell some of the typists under your supervision that the letters they prepare have too many errors, they contend that the letters are readable and that they obtain more satisfaction from their jobs if they do not have to be as concerned about errors.
These typists are
A. *correct*, because the ultimate objective should be job satisfaction
B. *incorrect*, because every job should be performed perfectly
C. *correct*, because they do not compose the letters themselves
D. *incorrect*, because their satisfaction is not the only consideration

15.____

16. Which of the following possible conditions is LEAST likely to represent a hindrance to effective communication?
A. The importance of a situation may not be apparent.
B. Words may mean different things to different people.
C. The recipient of a communication may respond to it, sometimes unfavorably
D. Communications may affect the self-interest of those communicating.

16.____

17. You are revising the way in which your unit handle records.
One of the BEST ways to make sure that the change will be implemented with a minimum of difficulty is to
A. allow everyone on the staff who is affected by the change to have an opportunity to contribute their ideas to the new procedures
B. advise only the key member of your staff in advance so that they can help you enforce the new method when it is implemented
C. give the assignment of implementation to the newest member of the unit
D. issue a memorandum announcing the change and stating that complaints will not be tolerated

17.____

18. One of your assistants is quite obviously having personal problems that are affecting his work performance.
As a supervisor, it would be MOST appropriate for you to
A. avoid any inquiry into the nature of the situation since this is not one of your responsibilities
B. avoid any discussion of personal problems on the basis that there is nothing you could do about them anyhow
C. help the employee obtain appropriate help with these problems
D. advise the employee that personal problems cannot be considered when evaluating work performance

18.____

19. The key to improving communication with your staff and other departments is the development of an awareness of the importance of communication.
Which of the following is NOT a good suggestion for developing this awareness?
    A. Be willing to look at your own attitude toward how you communicate
    B. Be sensitive and receptive to reactions to what you tell people
    C. Make sure all communication is in writing
    D. When giving your subordinates directions, try to put yourself in their place and see if your instructions still make sense

19.____

20. One of the assistants on your staff has neglected to complete an important assignment on schedule. You feel that a reprimand is necessary.
When speaking to the employee, it would usually be LEAST desirable to
    A. display your anger to show the employee how strongly you feel about the problem
    B. ask several questions about the reasons for failure to complete the assignment
    C. take the employee aside so that nobody else is present when you discuss the matter
    D. give the employee as much time as he needs to explain exactly what happened

20.____

KEY (CORRECT ANSWERS)

1.	D	11.	B
2.	B	12	A
3.	D	13.	D
4.	A	14.	B
5.	A	15.	D
6.	B	16.	C
7.	C	17.	A
8.	B	18.	C
9.	C	19.	C
10.	C	20.	A

EXAMINATION SECTION
TEST 1

DIRECTIONS: Each question or incomplete statement is followed by several suggested answers or completions. Select the one that BEST answers the question or completes the statement. *PRINT THE LETTER OF THE CORRECT ANSWER IN THE SPACE AT THE RIGHT.*

1. One of the things that can ruin morale in a work group is the failure to exercise judgment in the assignment of overtime work to your subordinates.
   Of the following, the MOST desirable supervisory practice in assigning overtime work is to
   A. rotate overtime on a uniform basis among all your subordinates
   B. assign overtime to those who are *moonlighting* after regular work hours
   C. rotate overtime as much as possible among employees willing to work additional hours
   D. assign overtime to those employees who take frequent long weekend vacations

2. The consistent delegation of authority by you to experienced and reliable subordinates in your work group is generally considered
   A. *undesirable*, because your authority in the group may be threatened by an unscrupulous subordinate
   B. *undesirable*, because it demonstrates that you cannot handle your own workload
   C. *desirable*, because it shows that you believe that you have been accepted by your subordinates
   D. *desirable*, because the development of subordinates creates opportunities for assuming broader responsibilities yourself

3. The MOST effective way for you to deal with a false rumor circulating among your subordinates is to
   A. have a trusted subordinate state a counter-rumor
   B. recommend disciplinary action against the rumor mongers
   C. point out to your subordinates that rumors degrade both listener and initiator
   D. furnish your subordinates with sufficient authentic information

4. Two of your subordinates tell you about a mistake they made in a report that has already been sent the top management.
   Which of the following questions is most likely to elicit the MOST valuable information from your subordinates?
   A. Who is responsible?
   B. How can we explain this to top management?
   C. How did it happen?
   D. Why weren't you more careful?

5. Assume that you are responsible for implementing major changes in work flow patterns and personnel assignments in the unit of which you are in charge. The one of the following actions which is MOST likely to secure the willing cooperation of those persons who will have to change their assignments?
   A. having the top administrators of the agency urge their cooperation at a group meeting
   B. issuing very detailed and carefully planned instructions to the affected employees regarding the changes
   C. integrating employee participation into the planning of the changes
   D. reminding the affected employees that career advancement depends upon compliance with organizational objectives

6. Of the following, the BEST reason for using face-to-face communication instead of written communication is that face-to-face communication
   A. allows for immediate feedback
   B. is more credible
   C. enables greater use of detail and illustration
   D. is more polite

7. Of the following, the MOST likely disadvantage of giving detailed instructions when assigning a task to a subordinate is that such instructions may
   A. conflict with the subordinate's ideas of how the task should be done
   B. reduce standardization of work performance
   C. cause confusion in the mind of the subordinate
   D. inhibit the development of new procedures by the subordinate

8. Assume that you are a supervisor of a unit consisting of a number of subordinates and that one subordinate, whose work is otherwise acceptable, keeps on making errors in one particular task assigned to him in rotation. This task consists of routine duties which all your subordinates should be able to perform.
   Of the following, the BEST way for you to handle this situation is to
   A. do the task yourself when the erring employee is scheduled to perform it and assign this employee other duties
   B. reorganize work assignments so that the task in question is no longer performed in rotation but assigned full-time to your most capable subordinate
   C. find out why this subordinate keeps on making the errors in question and see that he learns how to do the task properly
   D. maintain a well-documented record of such errors and, when the evidence is overwhelming, recommend appropriate disciplinary action

9. In the past, Mr. T, one of your subordinates, had been generally withdrawn and suspicious of others, but he had produced acceptable work. However, Mr. T has lately started to get into arguments with his fellow workers during which he displays intense rage. Friction between this subordinate and the others in your unit is mounting and the unit's work is suffering.

Of the following, which would be the BEST way for you to handle this situation?
- A. Rearrange work schedules and assignments so as to give Mr. T no cause for complaint
- B. Instruct the other workers to avoid Mr. T and not to respond to any abuse
- C. Hold a unit meeting and appeal for harmony and submergence of individual differences in the interest of work
- D. Maintain a record of incidents and explore with Mr. T the possibility of seeking professional help

10. You are responsible for seeing to it that your unit is functioning properly in the accomplishment of its budgeted goals.
Which of the following will provide the LEAST information on how well you are accomplishing such goals?
    - A. Measurement of employee performance
    - B. Identification of alternative goals
    - C. Detection of employee errors
    - D. Preparation of unit reports

11. Some employees see an agency training program as a threat.
Of the following, the MOST likely reason for such an employee attitude toward training is that the employee involved feel that
    - A. some trainers are incompetent
    - B. training rarely solves real work-a-day problems
    - C. training may attempt to change comfortable behavior patterns
    - D. training sessions are boring

12. Of the following, the CHIEF characteristic which distinguishes a good supervisor from a poor supervisor is the good supervisor's
    - A. ability to favorably impress others
    - B. unwillingness to accept monotony or routine
    - C. ability to deal constructively with problem situations
    - D. strong drive to overcome opposition

13. Of the following, the MAIN disadvantage of on-the-job training is that, generally,
    - A. special equipment may be needed
    - B. production may be slowed down
    - C. the instructor must maintain an individual relationship with the trainee
    - D. the on-the-job instructor must be better qualified than the classroom instructor

14. All of the following are correct methods for a supervisor to use in connection with employee discipline EXCEPT
    - A. trying not to be too lenient or too harsh
    - B. informing employees of the rules and the penalties for violations of the rules
    - C. imposing discipline immediately after the violation is discovered
    - D. making sure, when you apply discipline, that the employee understands that you do not want to do it

15. Of the following, the MAIN reason for a supervisor to establish standard procedures for his unit is to
    A. increase the motivation for his subordinates
    B. make it easier for the subordinates to submit to authority
    C. reduce the number of times that his subordinates have to consult him
    D. reduce the number of mistakes that his subordinates will make

16. Of the following, the BEST reason for using form letters in correspondence is that they are
    A. concise and businesslike
    B. impersonal in tone
    C. uniform in appearance
    D. economical for large mailings

17. The use of loose-leaf office manuals for the guidance of employees on office policy, organization, and office procedures has won wide acceptance.
    The MAIN advantage of the loose-leaf format is that it
    A. allows speedy reference
    B. facilitates revisions and changes
    C. includes a complete index
    D. presents a professional appearance

18. Office forms sometimes consist of several copies, each of a different color.
    The MAIN reason for using different colors is to
    A. make a favorable impression on the users of the form
    B. distinguish each copy from the others
    C. facilitate the appearance of legible carbon copies
    D. reduce cost, since using colored stock permits recycling of paper

19. Which of the following is the BEST justification for obtaining a photocopying machine for the office?
    A. A photocopying machine can produce an unlimited number of copies at a low fixed cost per copy.
    B. Employees need little training in operating a photocopying machine.
    C. Office costs will be reduced and efficiency increased.
    D. The legibility of a photocopy generally is superior to copy produced by any other office duplicating device.

20. Which one of the following should be the MOST important overall consideration when preparing a recommendation to automate a large-scale office activity?
    The
    A. number of models of automated equipment available
    B. benefits and costs of automation
    C. fears and resistance of affected employees
    D. experience of offices which have automated similar activities

21. A tickler file is MOST appropriate for filing materials
    A. chronologically according to date they were received
    B. alphabetically by name
    C. alphabetically by subject
    D. chronologically according to date they should be followed up

22. Which of the following is the BEST reason for decentralizing rather than centralizing the use of duplicating machines?
    A. Developing and retaining efficient duplicating machine operators
    B. Facilitating supervision of duplicating services
    C. Motivating employees to produce legible duplicated copies
    D. Placing the duplicating machines where they are most convenient and most frequently used

23. Window envelopes are sometimes considered preferable to individually addressed envelopes PRIMARILY because
    A. window envelopes are available in standard sizes for all purposes
    B. window envelopes are more attractive and official-looking
    C. the use of window envelopes eliminates the risk of inserting a letter in the wrong envelope
    D. the use of window envelopes requires neater typing

24. In planning the layout of a new office, the utilization of space and the arrangement of staff, furnishings and equipment should usually be MOST influenced by the
    A. gross square footage
    B. status differences in the chain of command
    C. framework of informal relationships among employees
    D. activities to be performed

25. When delegating responsibility for an assignment to a subordinate, it is MOST important that you
    A. retain all authority necessary to complete the assignment
    B. make yourself generally available for consultation with the subordinate
    C. inform your superiors that you are no longer responsible for the assignment
    D. decrease the number of subordinates whom you have to supervise

KEY (CORRECT ANSWERS)

1.	C	11.	C
2.	D	12.	C
3.	D	13.	B
4.	D	14.	D
5.	C	15.	C
6.	A	16.	D
7.	D	17.	B
8.	C	18.	B
9.	D	19.	C
10.	B	20.	B

21. D
22. D
23. C
24. D
25. B

TEST 2

DIRECTIONS: Each question or incomplete statement is followed by several suggested answers or completions. Select the one that BEST answers the question or completes the statement. *PRINT THE LETTER OF THE CORRECT ANSWER IN THE SPACE AT THE RIGHT.*

Questions 1-5.

DIRECTIONS: Questions 1 through 5 are to be answered on the basis of the following passage.

    The most effective control mechanism to prevent gross incompetence on the part of public employees is a good personnel program. The personnel officer in the line departments and the central personnel agency should exert positive leadership to raise levels of performance. Although the key factor is the quality of the personnel recruited, staff members other than personnel officers can make important contributions to efficiency. Administrative analysts, now employed in many agencies, make detailed studies of organization and procedures, with the purpose of eliminating delays, waste, and other inefficiencies. Efficiency is, however, more than a question of good organization and procedures; it is also the product of the attitudes and values of the public employees. Personal motivation can provide the will to be efficient. The best management studies will not result in substantial improvement of the performance of those employees who feel no great urge to work up to their abilities.

1. The passage indicates that the key factor in preventing gross incompetence of public employees is the
    A. hiring of administrative analysts to assist personnel people
    B. utilization of effective management studies
    C. overlapping of responsibility
    D. quality of the employees hired

2. According to the above passage, the central personnel agency staff should
    A. work more closely with administrative analysts in the line departments than with personnel officers
    B. make a serious effort to avoid jurisdictional conflicts with personnel officers in line departments
    C. contribute to improving the quality of work of public employees
    D. engage in a comprehensive program to change the public's negative image of public employees

3. The passage indicates that efficiency in an organization can BEST be brought about by
    A. eliminating ineffective control mechanisms
    B. instituting sound organizational procedures
    C. promoting competent personnel
    D. recruiting people with desire to do good work

4. According to the passage, the purpose of administrative analysis in a public agency is to
   A. prevent injustice to the public employee
   B. promote the efficiency of the agency
   C. protect the interests of the public
   D. ensure the observance of procedural due process

5. The passage implies that a considerable rise in the quality of work of public employees can be brought about by
   A. encouraging positive employee attitudes toward work
   B. controlling personnel officers who exceed their powers
   C. creating warm personal associations among public employees in an agency
   D. closing loopholes in personnel organization and procedures

6. Typist X can type 20 forms per hour and Typist I can type 30 forms per hour. If there are 30 forms to be typed and both typists are put to work on the job, how soon should they be expected to finish the work? _____ minutes.
   A. 32   B. 34   C. 36   D. 38

7. Assume that there were 18 working days in February and that the six clerks in your unit had the following number of absences:
   Clerk F – 3 absences
   Clerk G – 2 absences
   Clerk H – 8 absences
   Clerk I – 1 absence
   Clerk J – 0 absences
   Clerk K – 5 absences
   The average percentage attendance for the six clerks in your unit in February was MOST NEARLY
   A. 80%   B. 82%   C. 84%   D. 86%

8. A certain employee is paid at the rate of $15.00 per hour, with time-and-a-half for overtime. Hours in excess of 40 hours a week count as overtime. During the past week, the employee put in 48 working hours.
   The employee's gross wages for the week are MOST NEARLY
   A. $600   B. $700   C. $720   D. $840

9. You are making a report on the number of inside and outside calls handled by a particular switchboard. Over a 15-day period, the total number of all inside and outside calls handled by the switchboard was 5,760. The average number of inside calls per day was 234. You cannot find one day's tally of outside calls, but the total number of outside calls for the other fourteen days was 2,065. From this information, how many outside calls must have been reported on the missing tally?
   A. 175   B. 185   C. 195   D. 205

3 (#2)

10. A floor plan has been prepared for a new building, drawn to a scale of ¾ inch = 1 foot. A certain area is drawn 1 and ½ feet long and 6 inches wide on the floor plan.
What are the ACTUAL dimensions of this area in the new building?
_____ feet long and _____ feet wide.
    A. 21; 8   B. 24; 8   C. 27; 9   D. 30; 9

10.____

Questions 11-15.

DIRECTIONS: In answering Questions 11 through 15, assume that you are in charge of public information for an office which issues reports and answers questions from other offices and from the public on changes in land use. The following charts represent comparative land use in four neighborhoods. The area of each neighborhood is expressed in city blocks. Assume that all city blocks are the same size.

NEIGHBORHOOD A – 16 CITY BLOCKS   NEIGHBORHOOD B – 24 CITY BLOCKS

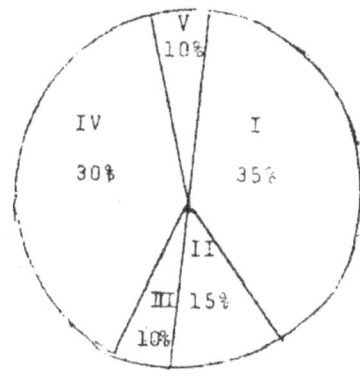 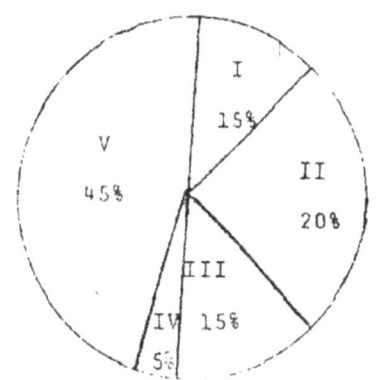

NEIGHBORHOOD C – 20 CITY BLOCKS   NEIGHBORHOOD D – 12 CITY BLOCKS

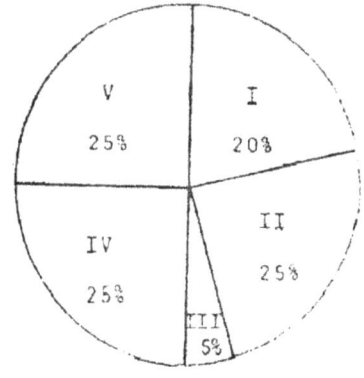 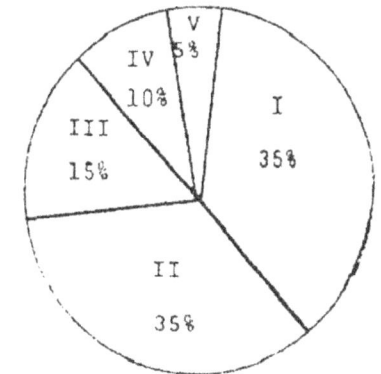

KEY: I: One- and two-family houses
      II: Apartment buildings
      III: Office buildings
      IV: Rental Stores
      V: Factories and warehouses

11. In how many of these neighborhoods does residential use (Categories I and 11.____
    II together) account for at least 50% of the land use?
    A. One   B. Two   C. Three   D. Four

12. Which neighborhood has the largest land area occupied by apartment 12.____
    buildings? Neighborhood
    A. A   B. B   C. C   D. D

13. In which neighborhood is the largest percentage of the land devoted to both 13.____
    office buildings and retail stores? Neighborhood _____.
    A. A   B. B   C. C   D. D

14. What is the difference, to the nearest city block, between the amount of land 14.____
    devoted to retail stores in Neighborhood B and the amount devoted to similar
    use in Neighborhood C? _____ block(s).

15. Which one of the following types of buildings occupies the same amount of 15.____
    land area in Neighborhood B as the amount of land area occupied by retail stores in
    Neighborhood A?
    A. 1   B. 2   C. 4   D. 6

Questions 16-20.

DIRECTIONS: Questions 16 through 20 are to be answered on the basis of the following passage.

For a period of nearly fifteen years, beginning in the mid-1960's, higher education sustained a phenomenal rate of growth. The factors principally responsible were continuing improvement in the rate of college entrance by high school graduates, a 50-percent increase in the size of the college-age (eighteen to twenty-one) group, and—until about 1977—a rapid expansion of university research activity supported by the federal government.

Today, as one looks ahead to the year 2030, it is apparent that each of these favorable stimuli will either be abated or turn into a negative factor. The rate of growth of the college-age group has already diminished, and from 2020 to 2025 the size of the college-age group will shrink annually almost as fast as it grew from 1975 to 1980. From 2025 to 2030, this annual decrease will slow down so that by 2030 the age-group will be about the same size as it was in 2029. This substantial net decrease in the size of the college-age group over the next fifteen years will dramatically affect college enrollments since, currently, 83 percent of undergraduates are twenty-one and under, and another 11 percent are twenty-one to twenty-four.

16. Which one of the following factors is NOT mentioned in the above passage as 16.____
    contributing to the high rate of growth of higher education?
    A. A larger increase in the size of the eighteen to twenty-one age group
    B. The equalization of educational opportunities among socio-economic groups
    C. The federal budget impact on research and development spending in the higher education sector
    D. The increasing rate at which high school graduates enter college

17. Based on the information in the above passage, the size of the college-age group in 2030 will be
    A. larger than it was in 2029
    B. larger than it was in 2015
    C. smaller than it was in 2025
    D. about the same as it was in 2020

18. According to the above passage, the tremendous rate of growth of higher education started around
    A. 1960   B. 1965   C. 1970   D. 1975

19. The percentage of undergraduates who are over age 24 is MOST NEARLY
    A. 6%   B. 8%   C. 11%   D. 17%

20. Which one of the following conclusions can be substantiated by the information given in the above passage?
    A. The college-age group will be about the same size in 2020 as it was in 1975.
    B. The annual decrease in the size of the college-age group from 2020 to 2025 will be about the same as the annual increase from 1975 to 1980.
    C. The overall decrease in the size of the college-age group from 2020 to 2025 will be followed by an overall increase in its size from 2025 to 2030.
    D. The size of the college-age group will decrease at a fairly constant rate from 2005 to 2020.

21. Because higher status is important to many employees, they will often make an effort to achieve it as an end in itself.
    Of the following, the BEST course of action for the supervisor to take on the basis of the preceding statement is to
    A. attach higher status to that behavior of subordinates which is directed toward reaching the goals of the organization
    B. avoid showing sympathy toward subordinates' wishes for increased wages, improved working conditions, or other benefits
    C. foster interpersonal competitiveness among subordinates so that personal friendliness is replaced by the desire to protect individual status
    D. reprimand subordinates whenever their work is in some way unsatisfactory in order to adjust their status accordingly

22. Assume that a large office in a certain organization operates long hours and is thus on two shifts with a slight overlap. Those employees, including supervisors, who are most productive are given their choice of shifts. The earlier shift is considered preferable by most employees.
    As a result of this method of assignment, which of the following is MOST likely to result?
    A. Most non-supervisory employees will be assigned to the late shift; most supervisors will be assigned to the early shift.
    B. Most supervisors will be assigned to the late shift; most non-supervisory employees will be assigned to the early shift.
    C. The early shift will be more productive than the late shift.
    D. The late shift will be more productive than the early shift.

23. Assume that a supervisor of a unit in which the employees are of average friendliness tells a newly-hired employee on her first day that her co-workers are very friendly. The other employees hear his remarks to the new employee. Which of the following is the MOST likely result of this action of the supervisor? The
    A. newly-hired employee will tend to feel less friendly than if the supervisor had said nothing
    B. newly-hired employee will tend to believe that her co-workers are very friendly
    C. other employees will tend to feel less friendly toward one another
    D. other employees will tend to see the newly-hired employee as insincerely friendly

23.____

24. A recent study of employee absenteeism showed that, although unscheduled absence for part of a week is relatively high for young employees, unscheduled absence for a full week is low. However, although full-week unscheduled absence is least frequent for the youngest employees, the frequency of such absence increases as the age of employees increases.
Which of the following statements is the MOST logical explanation for the greater full-week absenteeism among older employees?
    A. Older employees are more likely to be males.
    B. Older employees are more likely to have more relatively serious illnesses.
    C. Younger employees are more likely to take longer vacations.
    D. Younger employees are more likely to be newly-hired.

24.____

25. An employee can be motivated to fulfill his needs as he sees them. He is not motivated by what others think he ought to have, but what he himself wants. Which of the following statements follows MOST logically from the foregoing viewpoint?
    A. A person's different traits may be separately classified, but they are all part of one system comprising a whole person.
    B. Every job, however simple, entitles the person who does it to proper respect and recognition of his unique aspirations and abilities.
    C. No matter what equipment and facilities an organization has, they cannot be put to use except by people who have been motivated.
    D. To an observer, a person's need may be unrealistic but they ae still controlling.

25.____

KEY (CORRECT ANSWERS)

1. D
2. C
3. D
4. B
5. A

6. C
7. B
8. D
9. B
10. B

11. B
12. C
13. A
14. C
15. D

16. B
17. C
18. B
19. A
20. B

21. A
22. C
23. B
24. B
25. D

EXAMINATION SECTION
TEST 1

DIRECTIONS: Each question or incomplete statement is followed by several suggested answers or completions. Select the one that BEST answers the question or completes the statement. *PRINT THE LETTER OF THE CORRECT ANSWER IN THE SPACE AT THE RIGHT.*

1. Assume that you are a supervisor of a unit which is about to start work on an urgent job. One of your subordinates starts to talk to you about the urgent job but seems not to be saying what is really on his mind.
   What is the BEST thing for you to say under these circumstances?
   A. I'm not sure I understand. Can you explain that?
   B. Please come to the point. We haven't got all day.
   C. What is it? Can't you see I'm busy?
   D. Haven't you got work to do? What do you want?

   1._____

2. Assume that you have recently been assigned a new subordinate. You have explained to this subordinate how to fill out certain forms which will constitute the major portion of her job. After the first day, you find that she has filled out the forms correctly but has not completed as many as most other workers normally complete in a day.
   Of the following, the MOST appropriate action for you to take is to
   A. tell the subordinate how many forms she is expected to complete
   B. instruct the subordinate in the correct method filling out the forms
   C. monitor the subordinate's production to see if she improves
   D. reassign the job of filling out the forms to a more experienced worker in the unit

   2._____

3. One of the problems commonly met by the supervisor is the *touchy* employee who imagines slights when none are intended.
   Of the following, the BEST way to deal with such an employee is to
   A. ignore him, until he sees the error of his behavior
   B. frequently reassure him of his value as a person
   C. advise him that oversensitive people get promoted
   D. issue written instructions to him to avoid misinterpretation

   3._____

4. The understanding supervisor should recognize that a certain amount of anxiety is common to all newly-hired employees.
   If you are a supervisor of a unit and a newly-hired employee has been assigned to you, you can usually assume that the LEAST likely worry that the new employee has is worry about
   A. the job and the standards required in the job
   B. his acceptance by the other people in your unit
   C. the difficulty of advancing to top positions in the agency
   D. your fairness in evaluating his work

   4._____

5. In assigning work to subordinates, it is often desirable for you to tell them the overall or ultimate objective of the assignment.
   Of the following, the BEST reason for telling him the objective is that it will
   A. assure them that you know what you are doing
   B. eliminate most of the possible complaints about the assignment
   C. give them confidence in their ability to do the assignment
   D. help them to make decisions consistent with the objective

6. Generally a supervisor wishes to increase the likelihood that instructions given to subordinates will be carried out properly.
   Of the following, the MOST important action for the supervisor to take to accomplish this objective when giving instructions to subordinates is to
   A. tailor the instructions to fit the interests of the subordinate
   B. use proper timing in giving the instruction
   C. make sure that the subordinate understand the instructions
   D. include only those instructions that are essential to the task at hand

7. Suppose that a supervisor, because of his heavy workload, has decided to delegate to his subordinates some of the duties that he has been performing.
   Of the following attitudes of the supervisor, the one that is LEAST conducive toward effective delegation is his belief that
   A. his subordinates will make some mistakes in performing these duties
   B. controls will be necessary to make sure the work is done
   C. performance of these duties may be slowed down temporarily
   D. much of his time will be spent supervising performance of these duties

8. In attempting to determine why one of his subordinates has frequently been coming to work late, a supervisor begins an interview with the subordinate by asking her whether everything is all right on the job and at home.
   The BEST of the following reasons for beginning the interview in this manner is that a question specifically about the reason for the lateness
   A. might indicate insecurity on the part of the supervisor
   B. might limit the responses of the subordinate
   C. will offend the subordinate
   D. might reveal the purpose of the interview

9. Of the following, the BEST use to which a supervisor should put his knowledge of human relations is to
   A. enhance his image among his subordinates
   B. improve interpersonal relationships with the organization
   C. prompt the organization to awareness of mental health
   D. resolve technical difference of opinion among employees

10. Which of the following types of information would come tribute LEAST to a measure of the quality of working conditions for employees in various jobs?
    A. Data reflecting a view of working conditions as seen through the eyes of workers
    B. Objective data relating to problems in working conditions, such as occupational safety statistics

C. The considered opinion of recognized specialists in relevant fields
D. The impressionistic accounts of journalists in feature articles

Questions 11-15.

DIRECTIONS: Questions 11 through 15 each consist of a sentence which may or may not be an example of good English usage. Consider grammar, punctuation, spelling, capitalization, verbosity, awkwardness, etc. Examine each sentence, and then choose the correct statement about it from the four choices below it. If the English usage in the sentence is better as given than with any of the changes suggested in options B, C, or D, choose option A. Do NOT choose an option that will change the meaning of the sentence.

11. The clerk could have completed the assignment on time if he knows where these materials were located.
    A. This is an example of acceptable writing.
    B. The word *knows* should be replaced by *had known*.
    C. The word *were* should be replaced by *had been*.
    D. The words *where these materials were located* should be replaced by *the location of these materials*.

11.____

12. All employees should be given safety training. Not just those who have accidents.
    A. This is an example of acceptable writing.
    B. The period after the word *training* should be changed to a colon.
    C. The period after the word *training* should be changed to a semicolon, and the first letter of the word *Not* should be changed to a small *n*.
    D. The period after the word *training* should be changed to a comma, and the first letter of the word *Not* should be changed to a small *n*.

12.____

13. This proposal is designed to promote employee awareness of the suggestion program, to encourage employee participation in the program, and to increase the number of suggestions submitted.
    A. This is an example of acceptable writing.
    B. The word *proposal* should be spelled *proposal*.
    C. The words *to increase the number of suggestions submitted* should be changed to *an increase in the number of suggestions is expected*.
    D. The word *promote* should be changed to *enhance* and the word *increase* should be changed to *add to*.

13.____

14. The introduction of inovative managerial techniques should be preceded by careful analysis of the specific circumstances and conditions in each department.
    A. This is an example of acceptable writing.
    B. The word *techniques* should be spelled *techneques*.
    C. The word *inovative* should be spelled *innovative*.
    D. A comma should be placed after the word *circumstance* and after the word *conditions*.

14.____

15. This occurrence indicates that such criticism embarrasses him. 15.____
    A. This is an example of acceptable writing.
    B. The word *occurrence* should be spelled *occurence*.
    C. The word *criticism* should be spelled *criticizm*.
    D. The word *embarrasses* should be spelled *embarasses*.

Questions 16-18.

DIRECTIONS: Questions 16 through 18 each consist of four sentences. Choose the one sentence in each set of four that would be BEST for a *formal* letter or report. Consider grammar and appropriate usage.

16. A. Most all the work he completed before he become ill. 16.____
    B. He completed most of the work before becoming ill.
    C. Prior to him becoming ill his work was mostly completed.
    D. Before he became ill most of the work he had completed.

17. A. Being that the report lacked a clearly worded recommendation, it did not matter that it contained enough information. 17.____
    B. There was enough information in the report, although it, including the recommendation, were not clearly worded.
    C. Although the report contained enough information, it did not have a clearly worded recommendation.
    D. Though the report did not have a recommendation that was clearly worded, and the information therein contained was enough.

18. A. Having already overlooked the important mistake, the one which she found were not as important toward the end of the letter. 18.____
    B. Toward the end of the letter she had already overlooked the important mistake, so that which she had found were not as important.
    C. The mistakes which she had already overlooked were not as important as those which near the end of letter she had found.
    D. The mistakes which she found near the end of the letter were not as important as those which she had already overlooked.

19. Examine the following sentence, and then choose from below the words which should be inserted in the blank spaces to produce the BEST sentence. The unit has exceeded _____ goals and the employees are satisfied with _____ accomplishments. 19.____
    A. their; it's   B. it's; it's   C. its; there   D. its; their

20. Examine the following sentence, and then choose from below the words which should be inserted in the blank spaces to produce the BEST sentence. Research indicates that employees who _____ no opportunity for clos social relationships often find their work unsatisfying, and this _____ of satisfaction often reflects itself in low production. 20.____
    A. have; lack   B. have; excess   C. has; lack   D. has; excess

KEY (CORRECT ANSWERS)

1.	A	11.	B
2.	C	12.	D
3.	B	13.	A
4.	C	14.	C
5.	D	15.	A
6.	C	16.	B
7.	D	17.	C
8.	B	18.	D
9.	B	19.	D
10.	D	20.	A

TEST 2

DIRECTIONS: Each question or incomplete statement is followed by several suggested answers or completions. Select the one that BEST answers the question or completes the statement. *PRINT THE LETTER OF THE CORRECT ANSWER IN THE SPACE AT THE RIGHT.*

1. Of the following, the GREATEST *pitfall* in interviewing is that the result may be effected by the
    A. bias of the interviewee
    B. bias of the interviewer
    C. educational level of the interviewee
    D. educational level of the interviewer

    1.____

2. Assume that you have been asked to interview each of several students who have been hired to work part-time.
   Which of the following could *ordinarily* be accomplished LEAST effectively in such an interview?
    A. Providing information about the organization or institution in which the students will be working
    B. Directing the students to report for work each afternoon at specified times
    C. Determining experience and background of the students so that appropriate assignments can be made
    D. changing the attitudes of the students toward the importance of parental controls

    2.____

3. Assume that someone you are interviewing is reluctant to give you certain information.
   He would probably be MORE responsive if you show him that
    A. all the other persons you interviewed provided you with the information
    B. it would serve his own best interests to give you the information
    C. the information is very important to you
    D. you are businesslike and take a no-nonsense approach

    3.____

4. Taking notes while you are interviewing someone is MOST likely to
    A. arouse doubts as to your trustworthiness
    B. give the interviewee confidence in your ability
    C. insure that you record the facts you think are important
    D. make the responses of the interviewee unreliable

    4.____

5. Assume that you have been asked to get all the pertinent information from an employee who claims that she witnessed a robbery.
   Which of the following questions is LEAST likely to influence the witness's response?
    A. Can you describe the robber's hair?
    B. Did the robber have a lot of hair?
    C. Was the robber's hair black or brown?
    D. Was the robber's hair very dark?

    5.____

6. If you are to interview several applicants for jobs and rate them on five different factors on a scale of 1 to 5, you should be MOST careful to insure that your
   A. rating on one factor does not influence your rating on another factor
   B. ratings on all factors are interrelated with a minimum of variation
   C. overall evaluation for employment exactly reflects the arithmetic average of your ratings
   D. overall evaluation for employment is unrelated to your individual ratings

6.____

7. In answering questions asked by students, faculty, and the public, it is MOST important that
   A. you indicate your source of information
   B. you are not held responsible for the answers
   C. the facts you give be accurate
   D. the answer cover every possible aspect of each question

7.____

8. One of the applicants for a menial job is a tall, stooped, husky individual with a low forehead, narrow eyes, a protruding chin, and a tendency to keep his mouth open.
   In interviewing him, you SHOULD
   A. check him more carefully than the other applicants regarding criminal background
   B. disregard any skills he might have for other jobs which are vacant
   C. make your vocabulary somewhat simpler than with the other applicants
   D. make no assumption regarding his ability on the basis of his appearance

8.____

9. Of the following, the BEST approach for you to us at the beginning of an interview with a job applicant is to
   A. caution him to use his time economically and to get to the point
   B. ask him how long he intends to remain on the job if hired
   C. make some pleasant remarks to put him at ease
   D. emphasize the importance of the interview in obtaining the job

9.____

10. Of the following, the BEST reason for conducting an *exit interview* with an employee is to
    A. make certain that he returns all identification cards and office keys
    B. find out why he is leaving
    C. provide a useful training device for the exit interviewer
    D. discover if his initial hiring was in error

10.____

11. Suppose that a visitor to an office asks a receptionist for a specific person by name. The person is available, but the visitor refuses to state the purpose of the visit, saying that it is personal.
    Which of the following is the MOST appropriate response for the receptionist to make?
    A. Does M_____ know you?
    B. I'm sorry, M_____ is busy.
    C. M_____ won't be able to help you unless you're more specific.
    D. M_____ is not able to see you.

11.____

12. When writing a reply to a letter you received, it is proper to mention the subject of the letter.
    However, you should ordinarily NOT summarize the contents or repeat statements made in the letter you received PRIMARILY because
    A. a letter writer answers people, not letters
    B. direct answers will help you avoid sounding pompous
    C. the response will thus be more confidential
    D. the sender usually knows what he or she wrote

    12.____

13. Assume that you are a supervisor in an office which gets approximately equal quantities of urgent work and work that is not urgent. The volume of work is high during some periods and low during others.
    In order to level out the fluctuations in workload, it would be BEST for you to schedule work so that
    A. urgent work which comes up in a period of high work volume can be handled expeditiously by the use of voluntary overtime
    B. urgent work is postponed for completion in periods of low volume
    C. work is completed as it comes into the office, except that when urgent work arises, other work is laid aside temporarily
    D. work is completed chronologically, that is, on the basis of *first in, first out*

    13.____

14. Suppose that a supervisor sets up a pick-up and delivery messenger system to cover several nearby buildings. Each building has at least one station for both pick-up and delivery. Three messenger trips are scheduled for each day, and the messenger is instructed to make pick-up and deliveries at the same time.
    In this situation, telling the messenger to visit each pick-up and delivery station even though there is nothing to deliver to it is
    A. *advisable;* messengers are generally not capable of making decisions for themselves
    B. *advisable;* there may be material for the messenger to pick up
    C. *inadvisable;* the system must be made flexible to meet variable workload conditions
    D. *inadvisable;* postponing the visit until there is something to deliver is more efficient

    14.____

15. You, as a unit head, have been asked to submit budget estimates of staff, equipment and supplies in terms of programs for your unit for the coming fiscal year.
    In addition to their use in planning, such unit budget estimates can be BEST used to
    A. reveal excessive costs in operations
    B. justify increases in the debt limit
    C. analyze employee salary adjustments
    D. predict the success of future programs

    15.____

Questions 16-21.

DIRECTIONS: Questions 6 through 21 involve calculations of annual grade averages for college students who have just completed their junior year. These averages are to be based on the following table showing the number of credit hours for each student during the year at each of the grade levels: A, B, C, D, and F. How these letter grades may be translated into numerical grades is indicated in the first column of the table.

Grade Value	Credit Hours – Junior Year					
	King	Lewis	Martin	Nonkin	Ottly	Perry
A = 95	12	12	9	15	6	3
B = 85	9	12	9	12	918	6
C = 75	6	6	9	3	33	21
D = 65	3	3	3	3	6-	--
F = 0	-	--	3	-	--	--

Calculating a grade average for an individual student is a 4-step process:
I. Multiply each grade value by the number of credit hours for which the student received that grade.
II. Add these multiplication products for each student.
III. Add the student's total credit hours.
IV. Divide the multiplication product total by the total number of credit hours.
V. Round the result, if there is a decimal place, to the nearest whole number. A number ending in .5 would be rounded to the next higher number.

EXAMPLE

Using student King's grades as an example, his grade average can be calculated by going through the following four steps.

I. 95 x 12 = 1140
   85 x 9 = 765
   75 x 6 = 450
   65 x 3 = 195
   65 x 3 =   0

II. Total   2550

III. 12
     9
     6
     2
     0
     30 Total Credit Hours

IV. Divide 2550 by 30: $\frac{2550}{30}$ = 85

King's grade average is 85.

Questions 16 through 21 are to be answered on the basis of the information given above.

16. The grade average of Lewis is
    A. 83   B. 84   C. 85   D. 86

16._____

17. The grade average of Martin is 17.____
    A. 72 B. 73 C. 74 D. 75

18. The grade average of Nonkin is 18.____
    A. 85 B. 86 C. 87 D. 88

19. Student Ottly must attain a grade average of 90 in each of his years in 19.____
    college to be accepted into the graduate school of his choice.
    If, in summer school during his junior year, he takes two 3-credit courses and
    receives a grade of 95 in each one, his grade average for his junior year will
    then be MOST NEARLY
    A. 79 B. 80 C. 81 D. 82

20. If Perry takes an additional 3-credit course during the year and receives a grade 20.____
    of 95. his grade average will be increased to approximately
    A. 79 B. 80 C. 81 D. 82

21. What has been the effect of automation in data processing on the planning 21.____
    of managerial objectives?
    A. Paperwork can be virtually eliminated from the planning process.
    B. The information on which such planning is based can be more precise
       and up-to-date.
    C. Planning must be done much more frequently because of the constantly
       changing nature of the objectives.
    D. Planning can be done much less frequently because of the increased
       stability of objectives.

22. Which of the following is the BEST reason for budgeting a new calculating 22.____
    machine for an office?
    A. The clerks in the office often make mistakes adding.
    B. The machine would save time and money.
    C. It was budgeted last year but never received.
    D. All the other offices have calculating machines.

23. Which of the following is MOST likely to reduce the volume of paperwork in a 23.____
    unit responsible for preparing a large number of reports?
    A. Changing the office layout so that there will be a minimum of backtracking
       and delay
    B. Acquiring additional adding and calculating machines
    C. Consolidating some of the reports
    D. Inaugurating a *records retention policy* to reduce the length of time office
       papers are retained

24. With regard to typed correspondence received by most offices, which of the 24.____
    following is the GREATEST problem?
    A. Verbosity   B. Illegibility
    C. Improper folding   D. Excessive copies

25. Of the following, the GREATEST advantage of electronic typewriters over electric typewriters is that they usually
    A. are less expensive to repair
    B. are smaller and lighter
    C. produce better looking copy
    D. require less training for the typist

25.____

KEY (CORRECT ANSWERS)

1.	B		11.	A
2.	D		12.	D
3.	B		13.	C
4.	C		14.	B
5.	A		15.	A
6.	A		16.	C
7.	C		17.	D
8.	D		18.	C
9.	C		19.	B
10.	B		20.	B

21.	B
22.	B
23.	C
24.	A
25.	C

EFFECTIVELY INTERACTING WITH AGENCY STAFF AND MEMBERS OF THE PUBLIC

Test material will be presented in a multiple-choice question format.

Test Task: You will be presented with a variety of situations in which you must apply knowledge of how best to interact with other people.

SAMPLE QUESTION:

A person approaches you expressing anger about a recent action by your department.
Which one of the following should be your first response to this person?
- A. Interrupt to say you cannot discuss the situation until he calms down.
- B. Say you are sorry that he has been negatively affected by your department's action.
- C. Listen and express understanding that he has been upset by your department's action.
- D. Give him an explanation of the reasons for your department's action.

The CORRECT answer to this sample question is Choice C.
Solution:

Choice A is not correct. It would be inappropriate to interrupt. In addition, saying that you cannot discuss the situation until the person calms down will likely aggravate the person further.

Choice B is not correct. Apologizing for your department's action implies that the action was improper.

Choice C is the correct answer to this question. By listening and expressing understanding that your department's action has upset the person, you demonstrate that you have heard and understand the person's feelings and point of view.

Choice D is not correct. While an explanation of the reasons for the action may be appropriate at a later time, at this moment the person is angry and would not be receptive to such an explanation.

EXAMINATION SECTION
TEST 1

DIRECTIONS: Each question or incomplete statement is followed by several suggested answers or completions. Select the one that BEST answers the question or completes the statement. *PRINT THE LETTER OF THE CORRECT ANSWER IN THE SPACE AT THE RIGHT.*

1. Good procedure in handling complaints from the public may be divided into the following four principal stages:
   I. Investigation of the complaint
   II. Receipt of the complaint
   III. Assignment of responsibility for investigation and correction
   IV. Notification of correction

   The ORDER in which these stages ordinarily come is:
   A. III, II, I, IV   B. II, III, I, IV   C. II, III, IV, I   D. II, IV, III, I

   1.____

2. The department may expect the MOST severe public criticism if
   A. it asks for an increase in its annual budget
   B. it purchases new and costly street cleaning equipment
   C. sanitation officers and men are reclassified to higher salary grades
   D. there is delay in cleaning streets of snow

   2.____

3. The MOST important function of public relations in the department should be to
   A. develop cooperation on the part of the public in keeping streets clean
   B. get stricter penalties enacted for health code violations
   C. recruit candidates for entrance positions who ca be developed into supervisors
   D. train career personnel so that they can advance in the department

   3.____

4. The one of the following which has MOST frequently elicited unfavorable public comment has been
   A. dirty sidewalks or streets   B. dumping on lot
   C. failure to curb dogs   D. overflowing garbage cans

   4.____

5. It has been suggested that, as a public relations measure, sections hold *open house* for the public.
   The MOST effective time for this would be
   A. during the summer when children are not in school and can accompany their parents
   B. during the winter when show is likely to fall and the public can see snow removal preparations
   C. immediately after a heavy snow storm when department snow removal operations are in full progress
   D. when street sanitation is receiving general attention as during *Keep City Clean* week

   5.____

6. When a public agency conducts a public relations program, it is MOST likely to find that each recipient of its message will
   A. disagree with the basic purpose of the message if the officials are not well known to him
   B. accept the message if it is presented by someone perceived as having a definite intention to persuade
   C. ignore the message unless it is presented in a literate and clever manner
   D. give greater attention to certain portions of the message as a result of his individual and cultural differences

7. Following are three statements about public relations and communications:
   I.   A person who seeks to influence public opinion can speed up a trend
   II. Mass communications is the exposure of a mass audience to an idea
   III. All media are equally effective in reaching opinion leaders
   Which of the following choices CORRECTLY classifies the above statements into those which are correct and those which are not?
   A. I and II are correct, but III is not.
   B. II and III are correct, but I is not.
   C. I and III are correct, but II is not.
   D. III is correct, but I and II are not.

8. Public relations experts say that MAXIMUM effect for a message results from
   A. concentrating in one medium
   B. ignoring mass media and concentrating on *opinion makers*
   C. presenting only those factors which support a given position
   D. using a combination of two or more of the available media

9. To assure credibility and avoid hostility, the public relations man MUST
   A. make certain his message is truthful, not evasive or exaggerated
   B. make sure his message contains some dire consequence if ignored
   C. repeat the message often enough so that it cannot be ignored
   D. try to reach as many people and groups as possible

10. The public relations man MUST be prepared to assume that members of his audience
    A. may have developed attitudes toward his proposals—favorable, neutral, or unfavorable
    B. will be immediately hostile
    C. will consider his proposals with an open mind
    D. will invariably need an introduction to his subject

11. The one of the following statements that is CORRECT is:
    A. When a stupid question is asked of you by the public, it should be disregarded
    B. If you insist on formality between you and the public, the public will not be able to ask stupid questions that cannot be answered
    C. The public should be treated courteously, regardless of how stupid their questions may be
    D. You should explain to the public how stupid their questions are

12. With regard to public relations, the MOST important item which should be emphasized in an employee training program is that
    A. each inspector is a public relations agent
    B. an inspector should give the public all the information it asks for
    C. it is better to make mistakes and give erroneous information than to tell the public that you do not know the correct answer to their problem
    D. public relations is so specialized a field that only persons specially trained in it should consider it

12.____

13. Members of the public frequently ask about departmental procedures.
    Of the following, it is BEST to
    A. advise the public to put the question in writing so that he can get a proper formal reply
    B. refuse to answer because this is a confidential matter
    C. explain the procedure as briefly as possible
    D. attempt to avoid the issue by discussing other matters

13.____

14. The effectiveness of a public relations program in a public agency such as the authority is BEST indicated by the
    A. amount of mass media publicity favorable to the policies of the authority
    B. morale of those employees who directly serve the patrons of the authority
    C. public's understanding and support of the authority's program and policies
    D. number of complaint received by the authority from patrons using its facilities

14.____

15. In an attempt to improve public opinion about a certain idea, the BEST course of action for an agency to take would be to present the
    A. clearest statements of the idea even though the language is somewhat technical
    B. idea as the result of long-term studies
    C. idea in association with something familiar to most people
    D. idea as the viewpoint of the majority leaders

15.____

16. The fundamental factor in any agency's community relations program is
    A. an outline of the objectives
    B. relations with the media
    C. the everyday actions of the employees
    D. a well-planned supervisory program

16.____

17. The FUNDAMENTAL factor in the success of a community relations program is
    A. true commitment by the community
    B. true commitment by the administration
    C. a well-planned, systematic approach
    D. the actions of individuals in their contacts with the public

17.____

18. The statement below which is LEAST correct is:
    A. Because of selection standards, the supervisor frequently encounters problems resulting from subordinates' inability to express themselves in the language of the profession.
    B. Distortion of the meaning of a communication is usually brought about by a failure to use language that has a precise meaning to others.
    C. The term *filtering* is the distortion or dilution of content of a communication that occurs as information is passed from individual to individual.
    D. The complexity of the *communications net* will directly affect.

19. Consider the following three statements that may or may not be CORRECT:
    I. In order to prevent the stifling of communications flow, supervisors should insist that employees use the formal communications network.
    II. Two-way communications are faster and more accurate than one-way communications.
    III. There is a direct correlation between the effectiveness of communications and the total setting in which they occur.
    The choice below which MOST accurately describes the above statement is:
    A. All three are correct.
    B. All three are incorrect.
    C. More than one statement is correct.
    D. Only one of the statements is correct.

20. The statement below which is MOST inaccurate is:
    A. The supervisor's most important tool in learning whether or not he is communicating well is feedback.
    B. Follow-up is essential if useful feedback is to be obtained.
    C. Subordinates are entitled, as a matter of right, to explanations from management concerning the reasons for orders or directives.
    D. A skilled supervisor is often able to use the grapevine to good advantage.

21. *Since concurrence by those affected is not sought, this kind of communication can be issued with relative ease.*
    The kind of communication being referred to in this quotation is
    A. autocratic   B. democratic   C. directive   D. free-rein

22. The statement below which is LEAST correct is:
    A. Clarity is more important in oral communicating than in written since the readers of a written communication can read it over again.
    B. Excessive use of abbreviations in written communications should be avoided.
    C. Short sentences with simple words are preferred over complex sentences and difficult words in a written communication.
    D. The *newspaper* style of writing ordinarily simplifies expression and facilitates understanding.

23. Which one of the following is the MOST important factor for the department to consider in building a good public image?
    A. A good working relationship with the news media
    B. An efficient community relations program
    C. An efficient system for handling citizen complaints
    D. The proper maintenance of facilities and equipment
    E. The behavior of individuals in their contacts with the public.

24. It has been said that the ability to communicate clearly and concisely is the MOST important single skill of the supervisor.
    Consider the following statements:
    I. The adage, *Actions speak louder than words*, has NO application in superior/subordinate communications since good communications are accomplished with words.
    II. The environment in which a communication takes place will *rarely* determine its effect.
    III. Words are symbolic representations which must be associated with past experience or else they are meaningless.
    The choice below which MOST accurately describes the above statements is:
    A. I, II, and III are correct.
    B. I and II are correct, but III is not.
    C. I and III are correct, but II is not.
    D. III is correct, but I and II are not.
    E. I, II, and III are incorrect.

25. According to expert opinion, the effectiveness of an organization is very dependent upon good upward, downward, and lateral communications. Lateral communications are most important to the activity of coordinating the efforts of organizational units. Before real communication can take place at any level, barriers to communication must be recognized, understood, and removed.
    Consider the following three statements:
    I. The *principal* barrier to good communications is a failure to establish empathy between sender and receiver.
    II. The difference in status or rank between the sender and receiver of a communication may be a communications barrier.
    III. Communications are easier if they travel upward from subordinate to superior
    The choice below which MOST accurately describes the above statements is:
    A. I, II and III are incorrect.
    B. I and II are incorrect.
    C. I, II, and III are correct.
    D. I and II are correct.
    E. I and III are incorrect.

KEY (CORRECT ANSWERS)

1.	B	11.	C
2.	D	12.	A
3.	A	13.	C
4.	A	14.	C
5.	D	15.	C
6.	D	16.	C
7.	A	17.	D
8.	D	18.	A
9.	A	19.	D
10.	A	20.	C

21. A
22. A
23. E
24. D
25. E

EXAMINATION SECTION
TEST 1

DIRECTIONS: Each question or incomplete statement is followed by several suggested answers or completions. Select the one that BEST answers the question or completes the statement. *PRINT THE LETTER OF THE CORRECT ANSWER IN THE SPACE AT THE RIGHT.*

1. In public agencies, communications should be based PRIMARILY on a 1.____
   A. two-way flow from the top down and from the bottom up, most of which should be given in writing to avoid ambiguity
   B. multi-direction flow among all levels and with outside persons
   C. rapid, internal one-way flow from the top down
   D. two-way flow of information, most of which should be given orally for purposes of clarity

2. In some organizations, changes in policy or procedures are often communicated 2.____
   by word of mouth from supervisors to employees with no prior discussion or exchange of viewpoints with employees.
   This procedure often produces employee dissatisfaction CHIEFLY because
   A. information is mostly unusable since a considerable amount of time is required to transmit information
   B. lower-level supervisors tend to be excessively concerned with minor details
   C. management has failed to seek employees' advice before making changes
   D. valuable staff time is lost between decision-making and the implementation of decisions

3. For good letter writing, you should try to visualize the person to whom you are 3.____
   writing, especially if you know him.
   Of the following rules, it is LEAST helpful in such visualization to think of
   A. the person's likes and dislikes, his concerns, and his needs
   B. what you would be likely to say if speaking in person
   C. what you would expect to be asked if speaking in person
   D. your official position in order to be certain that your words are proper

4. One approach to good informal letter writing is to make letters and 4.____
   conversational.
   All of the following practices will usually help to do this EXCEPT:
   A. If possible, use a style which is similar to the style used when speaking
   B. Substitute phrases for single words (e.g., *at the present time* for *now*)
   C. Use contractions of words (e.g., *you're* for *you are*)
   D. Use ordinary vocabulary when possible

5. All of the following rules will aid in producing clarity in report-writing EXCEPT:
   A. Give specific details or examples, if possible
   B. Keep related words close together in each sentence
   C. Present information in sequential order
   D. Put several thoughts or ideas in each paragraph

6. The one of the following statements about public relations which is MOST accurate is that
   A. in the long run, appearance gains better results than performance
   B. objectivity is decreased if outside public relations consultants are employed
   C. public relations is the responsibility of every employee
   D. public relations should be based on a formal publicity program

7. The form of communication which is usually considered to be MOST personally directed to the intended recipient is the
   A. brochure   B. film   C. letter   D. radio

8. In general, a document that presents an organization's views or opinions on a particular topic is MOST accurately known as a
   A. tear sheet
   B. position paper
   C. flyer
   D. journal

9. Assume that you have been asked to speak before an organization of persons who oppose a newly announced program in which you are involved. You feel tense about talking to this group.
   Which of the following rules generally would be MOST useful in gaining rapport when speaking before the audience?
   A. Impress them with your experience
   B. Stress all areas of disagreement
   C. Talk to the group as to one person
   D. Use formal grammar and language

10. An organization must have an effective public relations program since, at its best, public relations is a bridge to change.
    All of the following statements about communication and human behavior have validity EXCEPT:
    A. People are more likely to talk about controversial matters with like-minded people than with those holding other views
    B. The earlier an experience, the more powerful its effect since it influences how later experiences will be interpreted
    C. In periods of social tension, official sources gain increased believability
    D. Those who are already interested in a topic are the ones who are most open to receive new communications about it

11. An employee should be encouraged to talk easily and frankly when he is dealing with his supervisor.
    In order to encourage such free communication, it would be MOST appropriate for a supervisor to behave in a(n)
    A. sincere manner; assure the employee that you will deal with him honestly and openly
    B. official manner; you are a supervisor and must always act formally with subordinates
    C. investigative manner; you must probe and question to get to a basis of trust
    D. unemotional manner; the employee's emotions and background should play no part in your dealings with him

12. Research findings show that an increase in free communication within an agency GENERALLY results in which one of the following?
    A. Improved morale and productivity
    B. Increased promotional opportunities
    C. An increase in authority
    D. A spirit of honesty

13. Assume that you are a supervisor and your superiors have given you a new-type procedure to be followed.
    Before passing this information on to your subordinates, the one of the following actions that you should take FIRST is to
    A. ask your superiors to send out a memorandum to the entire staff
    B. clarify the procedure in your own mind
    C. set up a training course to provide instruction on the new procedure
    D. write a memorandum to your subordinates

14. Communication is necessary for an organization to be effective.
    The one of the following which is LEAST important for most communication systems is that
    A. messages are sent quickly and directly to the person who needs them to operate
    B. information should be conveyed understandably and accurately
    C. the method used to transmit information should be kept secret so that security can be maintained
    D. senders of messages must know how their messages are received and acted upon

15. Which one of the following is the CHIEF advantage of listening willingly to subordinates and encouraging them to talk freely and honestly?
    It
    A. reveals to supervisors the degree to which ideas that are passed down are accepted by subordinates
    B. reduces the participation of subordinates in the operation of the department
    C. encourages subordinates to try for promotion
    D. enables supervisors to learn more readily what the *grapevine* is saying

16. A supervisor may be informed through either oral or written reports. 16.____
    Which one of the following is an ADVANTAGE of using oral reports?
    A. There is no need for a formal record of the report.
    B. An exact duplicate of the report is not easily transmitted to others.
    C. A good oral report requires little time for preparation.
    D. An oral report involves two-way communication between a subordinate and his supervisor.

17. Of the following, the MOST important reason why supervisors should 17.____
    communicate effectively with the public is to
    A. improve the public's understanding of information that is important for them to know
    B. establish a friendly relationship
    C. obtain information about the kinds of people who come to the agency
    D. convince the public that services are adequate

18. Supervisors should generally NOT use phrases like *too hard*, *too easy*, and 18.____
    a lot PRINCIPALLY because such phrases
    A. may be offensive to some minority groups
    B. are too informal
    C. mean different things to different people
    D. are difficult to remember

19. The ability to communicate clearly and concisely is an important element in 19.____
    effective leadership.
    Which of the following statements about oral and written communication is GENERALLY true?
    A. Oral communication is more time-consuming.
    B. Written communication is more likely to be misinterpreted.
    C. Oral communication is useful only in emergencies.
    D. Written communication is useful mainly when giving information to fewer than twenty people.

20. Rumors can often have harmful and disruptive effects on an organization. 20.____
    Which one of the following is the BEST way to prevent rumors from becoming a problem?
    A. Refuse to act on rumors, thereby making them less believable.
    B. Increase the amount of information passed along by the *grapevine*.
    C. Distribute as much factual information as possible.
    D. Provide training in report writing.

21. Suppose that a subordinate asks you about a rumor he has heard. The rumor 21.____
    deals with a subject which your superiors consider *confidential*.
    Which of the following BEST describes how you should answer the subordinate? Tell

A. the subordinate that you don't make the rules and that he should speak to higher ranking officials
B. the subordinate that you will ask your superior for information
C. him only that you cannot comment on the matter
D. him the rumor is not true

22. Supervisors often find it difficult to *get their message across* when instructing newly appointed employees in their various duties.
The MAIN reason for this is generally that the
    A. duties of the employees have increased
    B. supervisor is often so expert in his area that he fails to see it from the learner's point of view
    C. supervisor adapts his instruction to the slowest learner in the group
    D. new employees are younger, less concerned with job security and more interested in fringe benefits

22.____

23. Assume that you are discussing a job problem with an employee under your supervision. During the discussion, you see that the man's eyes are turning away from you and that he is not paying attention.
In order to get the man's attention, you should FIRST
    A. ask him to look you in the eye
    B. talk to him about sports
    C. tell him he is being very rude
    D. change your tone of voice

23.____

24. As a supervisor, you may find it necessary to conduct meetings with your subordinates.
Of the following, which would be MOST helpful in assuring that a meeting accomplishes the purpose for which it was called?
    A. Give notice of the conclusions you would like to reach at the start of the meeting.
    B. Delay the start of the meeting until everyone is present.
    C. Write down points to be discussed in proper sequence.
    D. Make sure everyone is clear on whatever conclusions have been reached and on what must be done after the meeting.

24.____

25. Every supervisor will occasionally be called upon to deliver a reprimand to a subordinate. If done properly, this can greatly help an employee improve his performance.
Which one of the following is NOT a good practice to follow when giving a reprimand?
    A. Maintain your composure and temper
    B. Reprimand a subordinate in the presence of other employees so they can learn the same lesson
    C. Try to understand why the employee was not able to perform satisfactorily
    D. Let your knowledge of the man involved determine the exact nature of the reprimand

25.____

KEY (CORRECT ANSWERS)

1.	C	11.	A
2.	B	12.	A
3.	D	13.	B
4.	B	14.	C
5.	D	15.	A
6.	C	16.	D
7.	C	17.	A
8.	B	18.	C
9.	C	19.	B
10.	C	20.	C

21.	B
22.	B
23.	D
24.	D
25.	B

TEST 2

DIRECTIONS: Each question or incomplete statement is followed by several suggested answers or completions. Select the one that BEST answers the question or completes the statement. *PRINT THE LETTER OF THE CORRECT ANSWER IN THE SPACE AT THE RIGHT.*

1. Usually one thinks of communication as a single step, essentially that of transmitting an idea.
   Actually, however, this is only part of a total process, the FIRST step of which should be
   A. the prompt dissemination of the idea to those who may be affected by it
   B. motivating those affected to take the required action
   C. clarifying the idea in one's own mind
   D. deciding to whom the idea is to be communicated

1.____

2. Research studies on patterns of informal communication have concluded that most individuals in a group tend to be passive recipients of news, while a few make it their business to spread it around in an organization.
   With this conclusion in mind, it would be MOST correct for the supervisor to attempt to identify these few individuals and
   A. give them the complete facts on important matters in advance of others
   B. inform the other subordinates of the identity of these few individuals so that their influence may be minimized
   C. keep them straight on the facts on important matters
   D. warn them to cease passing along any information to others

2.____

3. The one of the following which is the PRINCIPAL advantage of making an oral report is that it
   A. affords an immediate opportunity for two-way communication between the subordinate and superior
   B. is an easy method for the superior to use in transmitting information to others of equal rank
   C. saves the time of all concerned
   D. permits more precise pinpointing of praise or blame by means of follow-up questions by the superior

3.____

4. An agency may sometimes undertake a public relations program of a defensive nature.
   With reference to the use of defensive public relations, it would be MOST correct to state that it
   A. is bound to be ineffective since defensive statements, even though supported by factual data, can never hope to even partly overcome the effects of prior unfavorable attacks
   B. proves that the agency has failed to establish good relationships with newspapers, radio stations, or other means of publicity

4.____

87

2 (#2)

   C. shows that the upper echelons of the agency have failed to develop sound public relations procedures and techniques
   D. is sometimes required to aid morale by protecting the agency from unjustified criticism and misunderstanding of policies or procedures

5. Of the following factors which contribute to possible undesirable public attitudes towards an agency, the one which is MOST susceptible to being changed by the efforts of the individual employee in an organization is that
   A. enforcement of unpopular regulations as offended many individuals
   B. the organization itself has an unsatisfactory reputation
   C. the public is not interested in agency matters
   D. there are many errors in judgment committed by individual subordinates

5._____

6. It is not enough for an agency's services to be of a high quality; attention must also be given to the acceptability of these services to the general public.
   This statement is GENERALLY
   A. *false*; a superior quality of service automatically wins public support
   B. *true*; the agency cannot generally progress beyond the understanding and support of the public
   C. *false*; the acceptance by the public of agency services determines their quality
   D. *true*; the agency is generally unable to engage in any effective enforcement activity without public support

6._____

7. Sustained agency participation in a program sponsored by a community organization is MOST justified when
   A. the achievement of agency objectives in some area depends partly on the activity of this organization
   B. the community organization is attempting to widen the base of participation in all community affairs
   C. the agency is uncertain as to what the community wants
   D. the agency is uncertain as to what the community wants

7._____

8. Of the following, the LEAST likely way in which a records system may serve a supervisor is in
   A. developing a sympathetic and cooperative public attitude toward the agency
   B. improving the quality of supervision by permitting a check on the accomplishment of subordinates
   C. permit a precise prediction of the exact incidences in specific categories for the following year
   D. helping to take the guesswork out of the distribution of the agency

8._____

9. Assuming that the *grapevine* in any organization is virtually indestructible, the one of the following which it is MOST important for management to understand is:
   A. What is being spread by means of the *grapevine* and the reason for spreading it
   B. What is being spread by means of the *grapevine* and how it is being spread
   C. Who is involved in spreading the information that is on the *grapevine*
   D. Why those who are involved in spreading the information are doing so

10. When the supervisor writes a report concerning an investigation to which he has been assigned, it should be LEAST intended to provide
    A. a permanent official record of relevant information gathered
    B. a summary of case findings limited to facts which tend to indicate the guilt of a suspect
    C. a statement of the facts on which higher authorities may base a corrective or disciplinary action
    D. other investigators with information so that they may continue with other phases of the investigation

11. In survey work, questionnaires rather than interviews are sometimes used. The one of the following which is a DISADVANTAGE of the questionnaire method as compared with the interview is the
    A. difficulty of accurately interpreting the results
    B. problem of maintaining anonymity of the participant
    C. fact that it is relatively uneconomical
    D. requirement of special training for the distribution of questionnaires

12. in his contacts with the public, an employee should attempt to create a good climate of support for his agency.
    This statement is GENERALLY
    A. *false*; such attempts are clearly beyond the scope of his responsibility
    B. *true*; employees of an agency who come in contact with the public have the opportunity to affect public relations
    C. *false*; such activity should be restricted to supervisors trained in public relations techniques
    D. *true*; the future expansion of the agency depends to a great extent on continued public support of the agency

13. The repeated use by a supervisor of a call for volunteers to get a job done is objectionable MAINLY because it
    A. may create a feeling of animosity between the volunteers and the non-volunteers
    B. may indicate that the supervisor is avoiding responsibility for making assignments which will be most productive
    C. is an indication that the supervisor is not familiar with the individual capabilities of his men
    D. is unfair to men who, for valid reasons, do not, or cannot volunteer

14. Of the following statements concerning subordinates' expressions to a supervisor of their opinions and feelings concerning work situations, the one which is MOST correct is that
    A. by listening and responding to such expressions the supervisor encourages the development of complaints
    B. the lack of such expressions should indicate to the supervisor that there is a high level of job satisfaction
    C. the more the supervisor listens to and responds to such expressions, the more he demonstrates lack of supervisory ability
    D. by listening and responding to such expressions, the supervisor will enable many subordinates to understand and solve their own problems on the job

15. In attempting to motivate employees, rewards are considered preferable to punishment PRIMARILY because
    A. punishment seldom has any effect on human behavior
    B. punishment usually results in decreased production
    C. supervisors find it difficult to punish
    D. rewards are more likely to result in willing cooperation

16. In an attempt to combat the low morale in his organization, a high level supervisor publicized an *open-door policy* to allow employees who wished to do so to come to him with their complaints.
    Which of the following is LEAST likely to account for the fact that no employee came in with a complaint?
    A. Employees are generally reluctant to go over the heads of their immediate supervisor.
    B. The employees did not feel that management would help them.
    C. The low morale was not due to complaints associated with the job.
    D. The employees felt that they had more to lose than to gain.

17. It is MOST desirable to use written instructions rather than oral instructions for a particular job when
    A. a mistake on the job will not be serious
    B. the job can be completed in a short time
    C. there is no need to explain the job minutely
    D. the job involves many details

18. If you receive a telephone call regarding a matter which your office does not handle, you should FIRST
    A. give the caller the telephone number of the proper office so that he can dial again
    B. offer to transfer the caller to the proper office
    C. suggest that the caller re-dial since he probably dialed incorrectly
    D. tell the caller he has reached the wrong office and then hang up

19. When you answer the telephone, the MOST important reason for identifying yourself and your organization is to
    A. give the caller time to collect his or her thoughts
    B. impress the caller with your courtesy
    C. inform the caller that he or she has reached the right number
    D. set a business-like tone at the beginning of the conversation

    19._____

20. As soon as you pick up the phone, a very angry caller begins immediately to complain about city agencies and *red tape*. He says that he has been shifted to two or three different offices. It turs out that he is seeking information which is not immediately available to you. You believe, you know, however, where it can be found.
    Which of the following actions is the BEST one for you to take?
    A. To eliminate all confusion, suggest that the caller write the agency stating explicitly what he wants.
    B. Apologize by telling the caller how busy city agencies now are, but also tell him directly that you do not have the information he needs.
    C. Ask for the caller's telephone number and assure him you will call back after you have checked further.
    D. Give the caller the name and telephone number of the person who might be able to help, but explain that you are not positive he will get results/

    20._____

21. Which of the following approaches usually provides the BEST communication in the objectives and values of a new program which is to be introduced?
    A. A general written description of the program by the program manager for review by those who share responsibility
    B. An effective verbal presentation by the program manager to those affected
    C. Development of the plan and operational approach in carrying out the program by the program manager assisted by his key subordinates
    D. Development of the plan by the program manager's supervisor

    21._____

22. What is the BEST approach for introducing change?
    A
    A. combination of written and also verbal communication to all personnel affected by the change
    B. general bulletin to all personnel
    C. meeting pointing out all the values of the new approach
    D. written directive to key personnel

    22._____

23. Of the following, committees are BEST used for
    A. advising the head of the organization
    B. improving functional work
    C. making executive decisions
    D. making specific planning decisions

    23._____

24. An effective discussion leader is one who
    A. announces the problem and his preconceived solution at the start of the discussion
    B. guides and directs the discussion according to pre-arranged outline
    C. interrupts or corrects confused participants to save time
    D. permits anyone to say anything at any time

25. The human relations movement in management theory is basically concerned with
    A. counteracting employee unrest
    B. eliminating the *time and motion* man
    C. interrelationships among individuals in organizations
    D. the psychology of the worker

KEY (CORRECT ANSWERS)

1.	C		11.	A
2.	C		12.	B
3.	A		13.	B
4.	D		14.	D
5.	D		15.	D
6.	B		16.	C
7.	A		17.	D
8.	C		18.	B
9.	A		19.	C
10.	B		20.	C

21.	C
22.	A
23.	A
24.	B
25.	C

READING COMPREHENSION
UNDERSTANDING AND INTERPRETING WRITTEN MATERIAL
EXAMINATION SECTION
TEST 1

DIRECTIONS: Each question or incomplete statement is followed by several suggested answers or completions. Select the one that BEST answers the question or completes the statement. *PRINT THE LETTER OF THE CORRECT ANSWER IN THE SPACE AT THE RIGHT.*

Questions 1-5.

DIRECTIONS: Questions 1 through 5 are to be answered SOLELY on the basis of the following passage.

    The most effective control mechanism to prevent gross incompetence on the part of public employees is a good personnel program. The personnel officer in the line departments and the central personnel agency should exert positive leadership to raise levels of performance. Although the key factor is the quality of the personnel recruited, staff members other than personnel officers can make important contributions to efficiency. Administrative analysts, now employed in many agencies, make detailed studies of organization and procedures, with the purpose of eliminating delays, waste, and other inefficiencies. Efficiency is, however, more than a question of good organization and procedures; it is also the product of the attitudes and value of the public employees. Personal motivation can provide the will to be efficient. The best management studies will not result in substantial improvement of the performance of those employees who feel no great urge to wok up to their abilities.

1. The above passage indicates that the KEY factor in preventing gross incompetence of public employees is the
   A. hiring of administrative analysts to assist personnel people
   B. utilization of effective management studies
   C. overlapping of responsibility
   D. quality of the employees hired

   1.____

2. According to the above passage, the central personnel agency staff SHOULD
   A. work more closely with administrative analysts in the line departments than with personnel officers
   B. make a serious effort to avoid jurisdictional conflicts with personnel officers in line departments
   C. contribute to improving the quality of work of public employees
   D. engage in a comprehensive program to change the public's negative image of public employees

   2.____

3. The above passage indicates that efficiency in an organization can BEST be brought about by
   A. eliminating ineffective control mechanisms
   B. instituting sound organizational procedures
   C. promoting competent personnel
   D. recruiting people with desire to do good work

4. According to the above passage, the purpose of administrative analysts in a public agency is to
   A. prevent injustice to the public employee
   B. promote the efficiency of the agency
   C. protect the interests of the public
   D. ensure the observance of procedural due process

5. The above passage implies that a considerable rise in the quality of work of public employees can be brought about by
   A. encouraging positive employee attitudes toward work
   B. controlling personnel officers who exceed their powers
   C. creating warm personal associations among public employees in an agency
   D. closing loopholes in personnel organization and procedures

Questions 6-8.

DIRECTIONS: Questions 6 through 8 are to be answered SOLELY on the basis of the following passage.

EMPLOYEE NEEDS

The greatest waste in industry and in government may be that of human resources. This waste usually derives not from employees' unwillingness or inability, but from management's ineptness to meet the maintenance and motivational needs of employees. Maintenance needs refer to such needs as providing employees with safe places to work, written work rules, job security, adequate salary, employer-sponsored social activities, and with knowledge of their role in the overall framework of the organization. However, of greatest significance to employees are the motivational needs of job growth, achievement, responsibility, and recognition.

Although employee dissatisfaction may stem from either poor maintenance or poor motivation factors, the outward manifestation of the dissatisfaction may be very much like, i.e., negativism, complaints, deterioration of performance, and so forth. The improvement in the lighting of an employee's work area or raising his level of ay won't do much good if the source of the dissatisfaction is the absence of a meaningful assignment. By the same token, if an employee is dissatisfied with what he considers inequitable pay, the introduction of additional challenge in his work may simply make matters worse.

It is relatively easy for an employee to express frustration by complaining about pay, washroom conditions, fringe benefits, and so forth; but most people cannot easily express resentment in terms of the more abstract concepts concerning job growth, responsibility, and achievement.

It would be wrong to assume that there is no interaction between maintenance and motivational needs of employee. For example, conditions of high motivation often overshadow poor maintenance conditions. If an organization is in a period of strong growth and expansion, opportunities for job growth, responsibility, recognition, and achievement are usually abundant, but the rapid growth may have outrun the upkeep of maintenance factors. In this situation, motivation may be high, but only if employees recognize the poor maintenance conditions as unavoidable and temporary. The subordination of maintenance factors cannot go on indefinitely, even with the highest motivation.

Both maintenance and motivation factors influence the behavior of all employees, but employees are not identical and, furthermore, the needs of any individual do not remain orientation toward maintenance factors and those with greater sensitivity toward motivation factors.

A highly maintenance-oriented individual, preoccupied with the factors peripheral to his job rather than the job itself, is more concerned with comfort than challenge. He does not get deeply involved with his work but does with the condition of his work area, toilet facilities, and his time for going to lunch. By contrast, a strongly motivation-oriented employee is usually relatively indifferent to his surroundings and is caught up in the pursuit of work goals.

Fortunately, there are few people who are either exclusively maintenance-oriented or purely motivation-oriented. The former would be deadwood in an organization, while the latter might trample on those around him in his pursuit to achieve his goals.

6. With respect to employee motivational and maintenance needs, the management policies of an organization which is growing rapidly will probably result
    A. more in meeting motivational needs rather than maintenance needs
    B. more in meeting maintenance needs rather than motivational needs
    C. in meeting both of these needs equally
    D. in increased effort to define the motivational and maintenance needs of its employees

7. In accordance with the above passage, which of the following CANNOT be considered as an example of an employee maintenance need for railroad clerks?
    A. Providing more relief periods
    B. Providing fair salary increases at periodic intervals
    C. Increasing job responsibilities
    D. Increasing health insurance benefits

8. Most employees in an organization may be categorized as being interested in
    A. maintenance needs only
    B. motivational needs only
    C. both motivational and maintenance needs
    D. money only, to the exclusion of all other needs

Questions 9-11.

DIRECTIONS: Questions 9 through 11 are to be answered SOLELY on the basis of the following passage.

GOOD EMPLOYEE PRACTICES

As a city employee, you will be expected to take an interest in you work and perform the duties of your job to the best of your ability and in a spirit of cooperation. Nothing shows an interest in your work more than coming to work on time, not only at the start of the day but also when returning from lunch. If it is necessary for you to keep a personal appointment at lunch hour which might cause a delay in getting back to work on time, you should explain the situation to your supervisor and get his approval to come back a little late before you leave for lunch.

You should do everything that is asked of you willingly and consider important even the small jobs that your supervisor gives you. Although these jobs may seem unimportant, if you forget to do them or if you don't do them right, trouble may develop later.

Getting along well with your fellow workers will add much to the enjoyment of your work. You should respect your fellow workers and try to see their side when a disagreement arises. The better you get along with your fellow workers and your supervisor, the better you will like your job and the better you will be able to do it.

9. According to the above passage, in your job as a city employee, you are expected to
    A. show a willingness to cooperate on the job
    B. get your supervisor's approval before keeping any personal appointments at lunch hour
    C. avoid doing small jobs that seem unimportant
    D. do the easier jobs at the start of the day and the more difficult ones later on

9.____

10. According to the above passage, getting to work on time shows that you
    A. need the job
    B. have an interest in your work
    C. get along well with your fellow workers
    D. like your supervisor

10.____

11. According to the above passage, the one of the following statements that is NOT true is:
    A. If you do a small job wrong, trouble may develop
    B. You should respect your fellow workers
    C. If you disagree with a fellow worker, you should try to see his side of the story
    D. The less you get along with your supervisor, the better you will be able to do your job

11.____

Questions 12-15.

DIRECTIONS: Questions 12 through 15 are to be answered SOLELY on the basis of the following passage.

EMPLOYEE SUGGESTIONS

To increase the effectiveness of the city government, the city asks its employees to offer suggestions when they feel an improvement could be made in some government operation. The Employees' Suggestions Program was started to encourage city employees to do this. Through this Program, which is only for city employees, cash awards may be given to those whose suggestions are submitted and approved. Suggestions are looked for not only from supervisors but from all city employees as any city employee may get an idea which might be approved and contribute greatly to the solution of some problem of city government.

Therefore, all suggestions for improvement are welcome, whether they be suggestions on how to improve working conditions, or on how to increase the speed with which work is done, or on how to reduce or eliminate such things as waste, time losses, accidents or fire hazards. There are, however, a few types of suggestions for which cash awards cannot be given. An example of this type would be a suggestion to increase salaries or a suggestion to change the regulations about annual leave or about sick leave. The number of suggestions sent in has increased sharply during the past few years. It is hoped that it will keep increasing in the future in order to meet the city's needs for more ideas for improved ways of doing things.

12. According to the above passage, the MAIN reason why the city asks its employees for suggestions about government operations is to
    A. increase the effectiveness of the city government
    B. show that the Employees' Suggestion Program is working well
    C. show that everybody helps run the city government
    D. have the employee win a prize

13. According to the above passage, the Employees' Suggestion Program can approve awards ONLY for those suggestions that come from
    A. city employees
    B. city employees who are supervisors
    C. city employees who are not supervisors
    D. experienced employee of the city

14. According to the above passage, a cash award cannot be given through the Employees' Suggestion Program for a suggestion about
    A. getting work done faster
    B. helping prevent accidents on the job
    C. increasing the amount of annual leave for city employees
    D. reducing the chance of fire where city employees work

15. According to the above passage, the suggestions sent in during the past few years have
    A. all been approved
    B. generally been well written
    C. been mostly about reducing or eliminating waste
    D. been greater in number than before

Questions 16-18.

DIRECTIONS: Questions 16 through 18 are to be answered SOLELY on the basis of the following passage.

The supervisor will gain the respect of the members of his staff and increase his influence over them by controlling his temper and avoiding criticizing anyone publicly. When a mistake is made, the good supervisor will take it over with the employee quietly and privately. The supervisor will listen to the employee's story, suggest the better way of doing the job, and offer help so the mistake won't happen again. Before closing the discussion, the supervisor should try to find something good to say about other parts of the employee's work. Some praise and appreciation, along with instruction, is more likely to encourage an employee to improve in those areas where he is weakest.

16. A good title that would show the meaning of the above passage would be
    A. How to Correct Employee Errors
    B. How to Praise Employees
    C. Mistakes are Preventable
    D. The Weak Employee

17. According to the above passage, the work of an employee who has made a mistake is more likely to improve if the supervisor
    A. avoids criticizing him
    B. gives him a chance to suggest a better way of doing the work
    C. listens to the employee's excuses to see if he is right
    D. praises good work at the same time he corrects the mistake

18. According to the above passage, when a supervisor needs to correct an employee's mistake, it is important that he
    A. allow some time to go by after the mistake is made
    B. do so when other employee are not present
    C. show his influence with his tone of voice
    D. tell other employee to avoid the same mistake

Questions 19-23.

DIRECTIONS: Questions 19 through 23 are to be answered SOLELY on the basis of the following passage.

In studying the relationships of people to the organizational structure, it is absolutely necessary to identify and recognize the informal organizational structure. These relationships are necessary when coordination of a plan is attempted. They may be with *the boss*, line supervisors, staff personnel, or other representatives of the formal organization's hierarchy, and they may include the *liaison men* who serve as the leaders of the informal organization. An acquaintanceship with the people serving in these roles in the organization, and its formal counterpart, permits a supervisor to recognize sensitive areas in which it is simple to get conflict reaction. Avoidance of such areas, plus conscious efforts to inform other people of his own objectives for various plans, will usually enlist their aid and support. Planning *without* people can lead to disaster because the individuals who must act together to make any plan a success are more important than the plans themselves.

19. Of the following titles, the one that MOST clearly describes the above passage is
    A. Coordination of a Function
    B. Avoidance of Conflict
    C. Planning With People
    D. Planning Objectives

20. According to the above passage, attempts at coordinating plans may fail unless
    A. the plan's objectives are clearly set forth
    B. conflict between groups is resolved
    C. the plans themselves are worthwhile
    D. informal relationships are recognized

21. According to the above passage, conflict
    A. may, in some cases, be desirable to secure results
    B. produces more heat than light
    C. should be avoided at all costs
    D. possibilities can be predicted by a sensitive supervisor

22. The above passage implies that
    A. informal relationships are more important than formal structure
    B. the weakness of a formal structure depends upon informal relationships
    C. liaison men are the key people to consult when taking formal and informal structures into account
    D. individuals in a group are at least as important as the plans for the group

23. The above passage suggests that
    A. some planning can be disastrous
    B. certain people in sensitive areas should be avoided
    C. the supervisor should discourage acquaintanceships in the organization
    D. organizational relationships should be consciously limited

Questions 24-25.

DIRECTIONS: Questions 24 and 25 are to be answered SOLELY on the basis of the following passage.

Good personnel relations of an organization depend upon mutual confidence, trust, and good will. The basis of confidence is understanding. Most troubles start with people who do not understand each other. When the organization's intentions or motives are misunderstood, or when reasons for actions, practices, or policies are misconstrued, complete cooperation from individuals is not forthcoming. If management expects full cooperation from employees, it has a responsibility of sharing with them the information which is the foundation of proper understanding, confidence, and trust. Personnel management has long since outgrown the days when it was the vogue to *treat them rough and tell them nothing*. Up-to-date personnel management provides all possible information about the activities, aims, and purposes of the organization. It seems altogether creditable that a desire should exist among employees for such information which the best-intentioned executive might think would not interest them and which the worst-intentioned would think was none of their business.

24. The above passage implies that one of the causes of the difficulty which an organization might have with its personnel relations is that its employees
    A. have not expressed interest in the activities, aims, and purposes of the organization
    B. do not believe in the good faith of the organization
    C. have not been able to give full cooperation to the organization
    D. do not recommend improvements in the practices and policies of the organization

25. According to the above passage, in order for an organization to have good personnel relations, it is NOT essential that
    A. employees have confidence in the organization
    B. the purposes of the organization be understood by the employees
    C. employees have a desire for information about the organization
    D. information about the organization be communicated to employees

KEY (CORRECT ANSWERS)

1.	D		11.	D
2.	C		12.	A
3.	D		13.	A
4.	B		14.	C
5.	A		15.	D
6.	A		16.	A
7.	C		17.	D
8.	C		18.	B
9.	A		19.	C
10.	B		20.	D

21.	D
22.	D
23.	A
24.	B
25.	C

TEST 2

DIRECTIONS: Each question or incomplete statement is followed by several suggested answers or completions. Select the one that BEST answers the question or completes the statement. *PRINT THE LETTER OF THE CORRECT ANSWER IN THE SPACE AT THE RIGHT.*

Questions 1-8.

DIRECTIONS: Questions 1 through 8 are to be answered SOLELY on the basis of the following passage.

    Important figures in education and in public affairs have recommended development of a private organization sponsored in part by various private foundations which would offer installment payment plans to full-time matriculated students in accredited colleges and universities in the United States and Canada. Contracts would be drawn to cover either tuition and fees, or tuition, fees, room and board in college facilities, from one year up to and including six years. A special charge, which would vary with the length of the contract, would be added to the gross repayable amount. This would be in addition to interest at a rate which would vary with the income of the parents. There would be a 3% annual interest charge for families with total income, before income taxes, of $50,000 or less. The rate would increase by 1/10 of 1% for every $1,000 of additional net income in excess of $50,000 up to a maximum of 10% interest. Contracts would carry an insurance provision on the life of the parent or guardian who signs the contract; all contracts must have the signature of a parent or guardian. Payment would be scheduled in equal monthly installments.

1. Which of the following students would be eligible for the payment plan described in the above passage? A
   A. matriculated student taking six semester hours toward a graduate degree
   B. matriculated student taking seventeen semester hours toward an undergraduate degree
   C. graduate matriculated at the University of Mexico taking eighteen semester hours toward a graduate degree
   D. student taking eighteen semester hours in a special pre-matriculation program

1._____

2. According to the above passage, the organization described would be sponsored in part by
   A. private foundations   B. colleges and universities
   C. persons in the field of education   D. persons in public life

2._____

3. Which of the following expenses could NOT be covered by a contract with the organization described in the above passage?
   A. Tuition amounting to $20,000 per year
   B. Registration and laboratory fees
   C. Meals at restaurants near the college
   D. Rent for an apartment in a college dormitory

3._____

101

4. The total amount to be paid would include ONLY the
   A. principal
   B. principal and interest
   C. principal, interest, and special charge
   D. principal, interest, special charge, and fee

5. The contract would carry insurance on the
   A. life of the student
   B. life of the student's parents
   C. income of the parents of the student
   D. life of the parent who signed the contract

6. The interest rate for an annual loan of $25,000 from the organization described in the above passage for a student whose family's net income was $55,000 should be
   A. 3%   B. 3.5%   C. 4%   D. 4.5%

7. The interest rate for an annual loan of $35,000 from the organization described in the above passage for a student whose family's net income was $100,000 should be
   A. 5%   B. 8%   C. 9%   D. 10%

8. John Lee has submitted an application for the installment payment plan described in the above passage. John's mother and father have a store which grossed $500,000 last year, but the income which the family received from the store was $90,000 before taxes. They also had $5,000 income from stock dividends. They paid $10,000 in income taxes.
   The amount of income upon which the interest should be based is
   A. $85,000   B. $90,000   C. $95,000   D. $105,000

Questions 9-13.

DIRECTIONS: Questions 9 through 13 are to be answered SOLELY on the basis of the following passage.

Since the organization chart is pictorial in nature, there is a tendency for it to be drawn in an artistically balanced and appealing fashion, regardless of the realities of actual organizational structure. In addition to being subject to this distortion, there is the difficulty of communicating in any organization chart the relative importance or the relative size of various component parts of an organizational structure. Furthermore, because of the need for simplicity of design, an organization chart can never indicate the full extent of the interrelationships among the component parts of an organization.

These interrelationships are often just as vital as the specifications which an organization chart endeavors to indicate. Yet, if an organization chart were to be drawn with all the wide variety of criss-crossing communication and cooperation networks existent within a typical organization, the chart would probably be much more confusing than informative. It is also obvious that no organization chart as such can prove or disprove that the organizational structure it represents is effective in realizing the objectives of the organization. At best, an organization chart can only illustrate some of the various factors to be taken into consideration in understanding, devising, or altering organizational arrangements.

9. According to the above passage, an organization chart can be expected to portray the
    A. structure of the organization along somewhat ideal lines
    B. relative size of the organizational units quite accurately
    C. channels of information distribution within the organization graphically
    D. extent of the obligation of each unit to meet the organizational objectives

9.____

10. According to the above passage, those aspects of internal functioning which are NOT shown on an organization chart
    A. can be considered to have little practical application in the operations of the organization
    B. might well be considered to be as important as the structural relationships which a chart does present
    C. could be the cause of considerable confusion in the operations of an organization which is quite large
    D. would be most likely to provide the information needed to determine the overall effectiveness of an organization

10.____

11. In the above passage, the one of the following conditions which is NOT implied as being a defect of an organization chart is that an organization chart may
    A. present a picture of the organizational structure which is different from the structure that actually exists
    B. fail to indicate the comparative size of various organizational units
    C. be limited in its ability to convey some of the meaningful aspects of organizational relationships
    D. become less useful over a period of time during which the organizational facts which it illustrated have changed

11.____

12. The one of the following which is the MOST suitable title for the above passage is
    A. The Design and Construction of an Organization Chart
    B. The Informal Aspects of an Organization Chart
    C. The Inherent Deficiencies of an Organization Chart
    D. The Utilization of a Typical Organization Chart

12.____

13. It can be inferred from the above passage that the function of an organization chart is to
    A. contribute to the comprehension of the organization form and arrangements
    B. establish the capabilities of the organization to operate effectively
    C. provide a balanced picture of the operations of the organization
    D. eliminate the need for complexity in the organization's structure

13.____

Questions 14-16.

DIRECTIONS: Questions 14 through 16 are to be answered SOLELY on the basis of the following passage.

In dealing with visitors to the school office, the school secretary must use initiative, tact, and good judgment. All visitors should be greeted promptly and courteously. The nature of their business should be determined quickly and handled expeditiously. Frequently, the secretary should be able to handle requests, deliveries, or passes herself. Her judgment should determine when a visitor should see members of the staff or the principal. Serious problems or doubtful cases should be referred to a supervisor.

14. In general, visitors should be handled by the 14.____
    A. school secretary
    B. principal
    C. appropriate supervisor
    D. person who is free

15. It is wise to obtain the following information from visitors: 15.____
    A. Name
    B. Nature of business
    C. Address
    D. Problems they have

16. All visitors who wish to see members of the staff should 16.____
    A. be permitted to do so
    B. produce identification
    C. do so for valid reasons only
    D. be processed by a supervisor

Questions 17-19.

DIRECTIONS: Questions 17 through 19 are to be answered SOLELY on the basis of the following passage.

Information regarding payroll status, salary differentials, promotional salary increments, deductions, and pension payments should be given to all members of the staff who have questions regarding these items. On occasion, if the secretary is uncertain regarding the information, the staff member should be referred to the principal or the appropriate agency. No question by a staff member regarding payroll status should be brushed aside as immaterial or irrelevant. The school secretary must always try to handle the question or pass it on to the person who can handle it.

17. If a teacher is dissatisfied with information regarding her salary status, as given by the school secretary, the matter should be 17.____
    A. dropped
    B. passed on to the principal
    C. passed on by the secretary to proper agency or the principal
    D. made a basis for grievance procedures

18. The following is an adequate summary of the above passage: 18.____
    A. The secretary must handle all payroll matters
    B. The secretary must handle all payroll matter or know who can handle them
    C. The secretary or the principal must handle all payroll matters
    D. Payroll matter too difficult to handle must be followed up until they are solved

19. The above passage implies that
    A. many teachers ask immaterial questions regarding payroll status
    B. few teachers ask irrelevant pension questions
    C. no teachers ask immaterial salary questions
    D. no question regarding salary should be considered irrelevant

19._____

Questions 20-22.

DIRECTIONS: Questions 20 through 22 are to be answered SOLELY on the basis of the following passage.

The necessity for good speech on the part of the school secretary cannot be overstated. The school secretary must deal with the general public, the pupils, the members of the staff, and the school supervisors. In every situation which involves the general public, the secretary serves as a representative of the school. In dealing with pupils, the secretary's speech must serve as a model from which students may guide themselves. Slang, colloquialisms, malapropisms, and local dialects must be avoided.

20. The above passage implies that the speech pattern of the secretary must be
    A. perfect   B. very good
    C. average   D. on a level with that of the pupils

20._____

21. The last sentence indicates that slang
    A. is acceptable   B. occurs in all speech
    C. might be used occasionally D. should be shunned

21._____

22. The above passage implies that the speech of pupils
    A. may be influenced   B. does not change readily
    C. is generally good   D. is generally poor

22._____

Questions 23-25.

DIRECTIONS: Questions 23 through 25 are to be answered SOLELY on the basis of the following passage.

The school secretary who is engaged in the task of filing records and correspondence should follow a general set of rules. Items which are filed should be available to other secretaries or to supervisors quickly and easily by means of the application of a modicum of common sense and good judgment. Items which, by their nature, may be difficult to find should be cross-indexed. Folders and drawers should be neatly and accurately labeled. There should never be a large accumulation of papers which have not been filed.

23. A good general rule to follow in filing is that materials should be
    A. placed in folders quickly   B. neatly stored
    C. readily available   D. cross-indexed

23._____

24. Items that are filed should be available to
    A. the secretary charged with the task of filing
    B. secretaries and supervisors
    C. school personnel
    D. the principal

    24.____

25. A modicum of common sense means _____ common sense.
    A. an average amount of
    B. a great deal of
    C. a little
    D. no

    25.____

KEY (CORRECT ANSWERS)

1.	B		11.	D
2.	A		12.	C
3.	C		13.	A
4.	C		14.	A
5.	D		15.	B
6.	B		16.	C
7.	B		17.	C
8.	C		18.	B
9.	A		19.	D
10.	B		20.	B

21.	D
22.	A
23.	C
24.	B
25.	C

TEST 3

DIRECTIONS: Each question or incomplete statement is followed by several suggested answers or completions. Select the one that BEST answers the question or completes the statement. *PRINT THE LETTER OF THE CORRECT ANSWER IN THE SPACE AT THE RIGHT.*

Questions 1-4.

DIRECTIONS: Questions 1 through 4 are to be answered SOLELY on the basis of the following passage.

The proposition that administrative activity is essentially the same in all organizations appears to underlie some of the practices in the administration of private higher education. Although the practice is unusual in public education, there are numerous instances of industrial, governmental, or military administrators being assigned to private institutions of higher education and, to a lesser extent, of college and university presidents assuming administrative positions in other types of organizations. To test this theory that administrators are interchangeable, there is a need for systematic observation and classification. The myth that an educational administrator must first have experience in the teaching profession is firmly rooted in a long tradition that has historical prestige. The myth is bound up in the expectations of the public and personnel surrounding the administrator. Since administrative success depends significantly on how well an administrator meets the expectations others have of him, the myth may be more powerful than the special experience in helping the administrator attain organizational and educational objectives. Educational administrators who have risen through the teaching profession have often expressed nostalgia for the life of a teacher or scholar, but there is no evidence that this nostalgia contributes to administrative success.

1. Which of the following statements as completed is MOST consistent with the above passage?
   The greatest number of administrators has moved from
   A. industry and the military to government and universities
   B. government and universities to industry and the military
   C. government, the armed forces, and industry to colleges and universities
   D. colleges and universities to government, the armed forces, and industry

1.____

2. Of the following, the MOST reasonable inference from the above passage is that a specific area requiring further research is the
   A. place of myth in the tradition and history of the educational profession
   B. relative effectiveness of educational administrators from inside and outside the teaching profession
   C. performance of administrators in the administration of public colleges
   D. degree of reality behind the nostalgia for scholarly pursuits often expressed by educational administrators

2.____

3. According to the above passage, the value to an educational administrator of experience in the teaching profession
   A. lies in the first-hand knowledge he has acquired of immediate educational problems
   B. may lie in the belief of his colleagues, subordinates, and the public that such experience is necessary
   C. has been supported by evidence that the experience contributes to administrative success in educational fields
   D. would be greater if the administrator were able to free himself from nostalgia for his former duties

3._____

4. Of the following, the MOST suitable title for the above passage is
   A. Educational Administration, Its Problems
   B. The Experience Needed For Educational Administration
   C. Administration in Higher Education
   D. Evaluating Administrative Experience

4._____

Questions 5-6.

DIRECTIONS: Questions 5 and 6 are to be answered SOLELY on the basis of the following passage.

Management by objectives (MBO) may be defined as the process by which the superior and the subordinate managers of an organization jointly define its common goals, define each individual's major areas of responsibility in terms of the results expected of him and use these measure as guides for operating the unit and assessing the contribution of each of its members.

The MBO approach requires that after organizational goals are established and communicated, targets must be set for each individual position which are congruent with organizational goals. Periodic performance reviews and a final review using the objectives set as criteria are also basic to this approach.

Recent studies have shown that MBO programs are influenced by attitudes and perceptions of the boss, the company, the reward-punishment system, and the program itself. In addition, the manner in which the MBO program is carried out can influence the success of the program. A study done in the late sixties indicates that the best results are obtained when the manager sets goals which deal with significant problem areas in the organizational unit, or with the subordinate's personal deficiencies. These goals must be clear with regard to what is expected of the subordinate. The frequency of feedback is also important in the success of a management-by-objectives program. Generally, the greater the amount of feedback, the more successful the MBO program.

5. According to the above passage, the expected output for individual employees should be determined
   A. after a number of reviews of work performance
   B. after common organizational goals are defined
   C. before common organizational goals are defined
   D. on the basis of an employee's personal qualities

5._____

6. According to the above passage, the management-by-objectives approach requires
   A. less feedback than other types of management programs
   B. little review of on-the-job performance after the initial setting of goals
   C. general conformance between individual goals and organizational goals
   D. the setting of goals which deal with minor problem areas in the organization

6._____

Questions 7-10.

DIRECTIONS: Questions 7 through 10 are to be answered SOLELY on the basis of the following passage.

   Management, which is the function of executive leadership, has as its principal phases the planning, organizing, and controlling of the activities of subordinate groups in the accomplishment of organizational objectives. Planning specifies the kind and extent of the factors, forces, and effects, and the relationships among them, that will be required for satisfactory accomplishment. The nature of the objectives and their requirements must be known before determinations can be made as to what must be done, how it must be done and why, where actions should take place, who should be responsible, and similar programs pertaining to the formulation of a plan. Organizing, which creates the conditions that must be present before the execution of the plan can be undertaken successfully, cannot be done intelligently without knowledge of the organizational objectives. Control, which has to do with the constraint and regulation of activities entering into the execution of the plan, must be exercised in accordance with the characteristics and requirements of the activities demanded by the plan.

7. The one of the following which is the MOST suitable title for the above passage is
   A. The Nature of Successful Organization
   B. The Planning of Management Functions
   C. The Importance of Organizational Functions
   D. The Principle Aspects of Management

7._____

8. It can be inferred from the above passage that the one of the following functions whose existence is essential to the existence of the other three is the
   A. regulation of the work needed to carry out a plan
   B. understanding of what the organization intends to accomplish
   C. securing of information of the factors necessary for accomplishment of objectives
   D. establishment of the conditions required for successful action

8._____

9. The one of the following which would NOT be included within any of the principal phases of the function of executive leadership as defined in the above passage is
   A. determination of manpower requirements
   B. procurement of required material
   C. establishment of organizational objectives
   D. scheduling of production

9._____

10. The conclusion which can MOST reasonably be drawn from the above passage is that the control phase of managing is most directly concerned with the
    A. influencing of policy determinations
    B. administering of suggestion systems
    C. acquisition of staff for the organization
    D. implementation of performance standards

10._____

Questions 11-12.

DIRECTIONS: Questions 11 and 12 are to be answered SOLELY on the basis of the following passage.

Under an open-and-above-board policy, it is to be expected that some supervisors will gloss over known shortcomings of subordinates rather than face the task of discussing team face-to-face. It is also to be expected that at least some employees whose job performance is below par will reject the supervisor's appraisal as biased and unfair. Be that as it may, these are inescapable aspects of any performance appraisal system in which human beings are involved. The supervisor who shies away from calling a spade a spade, as well as the employee with a chip on his shoulder, will each in his own way eventually be revealed in his true light—to the benefit of the organization as a whole.

11. The BEST of the following interpretations of the above passage is that
    A. the method of rating employee performance requires immediate revision to improve employee acceptance
    B. substandard performance ratings should be discussed with employees even if satisfactory ratings are not
    C. supervisors run the risk of being called unfair by the subordinates even though their appraisals are accurate
    D. any system of employee performance rating is satisfactory if used properly

11._____

12. The BEST of the following interpretations of the above passage is that
    A. supervisors generally are not open-and-above-board with their subordinates
    B. it is necessary for supervisors to tell employees objectively how they are performing
    C. employees complain when their supervisor does not keep them informed
    D. supervisors are afraid to tell subordinates their weaknesses

12._____

Questions 13-15.

DIRECTIONS: Questions 13 through 15 are to be answered SOLELY on the basis of the following passage.

During the last decade, a great deal of interest has been generated around the phenomenon of *organizational development,* or the process of developing human resources through conscious organization effort. Organizational development (OD) stresses improving interpersonal relationships and organizational skills, such as communication, to a much greater degree than individual training ever did. The kind of training that an organization should emphasize depends upon the present and future structure of the organization. If future organizations are to be unstable, shifting coalitions, then individual skills and abilities, particularly those emphasizing innovativeness, creativity, flexibility, and the latest technological knowledge, are crucial and individual training is most appropriate.

But if there is to be little change in organizational structure, then the main thrust of training should be group-oriented or organizational development. This approach seems better designed for overcoming hierarchical barriers, for developing a degree of interpersonal relationships which make communication along the chain of command possible, and for retaining a modicum of innovation and/or flexibility.

13. According to the above passage, group-oriented training is MOST useful in in
    A. developing a communications system that will facilitate understanding through the chain of command
    B. highly flexible and mobile organizations
    C. preventing the crossing of hierarchical barriers within an organization
    D. saving energy otherwise wasted on developing methods of dealing with rigid hierarchies

14. The one of the following conclusions which can be drawn MOST appropriately from the above passage is that
    A. behavioral research supports the use of organizational development training methods rather than individualized training
    B. it is easier to provide individualized training in specific skills than to set up sensitivity training programs
    C. organizational development eliminates innovative or flexible activity
    D. the nature of an organization greatly influences which training methods will be most effective

15. According to the above passage, the one of the following which is LEAST important for large-scale organizations geared to rapid and abrupt change is
    A. current technological information
    B. development of a high degree of interpersonal relationships
    C. development of individual skills and abilities
    D. emphasis on creativity

Questions 16-18.

DIRECTIONS: Questions 16 through 18 are to be answered SOLELY on the basis of the following passage.

The increase in the extent to which each individual is personally responsible to others is most noticeable in a large bureaucracy. No one person *decides* anything; each decision of any importance, is the product of an intricate process of brokerage involving individuals inside and outside the organization who feel some reason to be affected by the decision, or two have special knowledge to contribute to it. The more varied the organization's constituency, the more inside *veto-groups* will need to be taken into account. But even if no outside consultations were involved, sheer size would produce a complex process of decision. For a large organization is a deliberately created system of tensions into which each individual is expected to bring work-ways, viewpoints, and outside relationships markedly different from those of his colleagues. It is the administrator's task to draw from these disparate forces the elements of wise action from day to day, consistent with the purposes of the organization as a whole.

16. The above passage is essentially a description of decision-making as 16.____
    A. an organization process
    B. the key responsibility of the administrator
    C. the one best position among many
    D. a complex of individual decisions

17. Which one of the following statements BEST describes the responsibilities of 17.____
    an administrator?
    A. He modifies decisions and goals in accordance with pressures from within and outside the organization.
    B. He creates problem-solving mechanisms that rely on the varied interests of his staff and *veto-groups*.
    C. He makes determinations that will lead to attainment of his agency's objectives.
    D. He obtains agreement among varying viewpoints and interests

18. In the context of the operations of a central public personnel agency, a 18.____
    veto-group would LEAST likely consist of
    A. employee organizations
    B. professional personnel societies
    C. using agencies
    D. civil service newspapers

Questions 19-25.

DIRECTIONS: Questions 19 through 25 are to be answered SOLELY on the basis of the following passage, which is an extract from a report prepared for Department X, which outlines the procedure to be followed in the case of transfers of employees.

Every transfer, regardless of the reason therefore, requires completion of the record of transfer, Form DT411. To denote consent to the transfer, DT411 should contain the signatures of the transferee and the personnel officer(s) concerned, except that, in the case of an involuntary transfer, the signatures of the transferee's present and prospective supervisors shall be entered in Boxes 8A and 8B, respectively, since the transferee does not consent. Only a permanent employee may request a transfer; in such cases, the employee's attendance record shall be duly considered with regard to absences, latenesses, and accrued overtime balances. In the case of an inter-district transfer, the employee's attendance record must be included in Section 8A of the transfer request, Form DT410, by the personnel officer of the district from which the transfer is requested. The personnel officer of the district to which the employee requested transfer may refuse to accept accrued overtime balances in excess of ten days.

An employee on probation shall be eligible for transfer. If such employee is involuntarily transferred, he shall be credited for the period of time already served on probation. However, if such transfer is voluntary, the employee shall be required to serve the entire period of his probation in the new position. An employee who has occurred a disability which prevents him from performing his normal duties may be transferred during the period of such disability to other appropriate duties. A disability transfer requires the completion of either DT414 if the disability is job-connected, or Form DT415 if it is not a job-connected disability. In either case, the personnel officer of the district from which the transfer is made signs in Box 6A of the first two copies and the personnel officer of the district to which the transfer is made signs in Box 6B of the last two copies, or, in the case of an intra-district disability transfer, the personnel officer must sign in Box 6A of the first two copies and Box 6B of the last two copies.

19. When a personnel officer consents to an employee's request for transfer from his district, this procedure requires that the personnel officer sign Forms
    A. DT411
    B. DT410 and DT411
    C. DT411 and either Form DT414 or DT415
    D. DT410 and DT411, and either Form DT414 or DT415

20. With respect to the time record of an employee transferred against his wishes during his probationary period, this procedure requires that
    A. he serve the entire period of his probation in his present office
    B. he lose his accrued overtime balance
    C. his attendance record be considered with regard to absences and latenesses
    D. he be given credit for the period of time he has already served on probation

21. Assume you are a supervisor and an employee must be transferred into your office against his wishes.
    According to this procedure, the box you must sign on the record of transfer is
    A. 6A   B. 8A   C. 6B   D. 8B

22. Under this procedure, in the case of a disability transfer, when must Box 6A on Forms DT414 and DT415 be signed by the personnel officer of the district to which the transfer is being made?
    A. In all cases when either Form DT414 or Form DT415 is used
    B. In all cases when Form DT414 is used and only under certain circumstances when Form DT415 is used
    C. In all cases when Form DT415 is used and only under certain circumstances when Form DT414 is used
    D. Only under certain circumstances when either Form DT414 or Form DT415 is used

23. From the above passage, it may be inferred MOST correctly that the number of copies of Form DT414 is
    A. no more than 2
    B. at least 3
    C. at least 5
    D. more than the number of copies of Form DT415

23.____

24. A change in punctuation and capitalization only which would change one sentence into two and possibly contribute to somewhat greater ease of reading this report extract would be MOST appropriate in the
    A. 2nd sentence, 1st paragraph
    B. 3rd sentence, 1st paragraph
    C. next to the last sentence, 2nd paragraph
    D. 2nd sentence, 2nd paragraph

24.____

25. In the second paragraph, a word that is INCORRECTLY used is
    A. *shall* in the 1st sentence
    B. *voluntary* in the 3rd sentence
    C. *occurred* in the 4th sentence
    D. *intra-district* in the last sentence

25.____

KEY (CORRECT ANSWERS)

1.	C		11.	C
2.	B		12.	B
3.	B		13.	A
4.	B		14.	D
5.	B		15.	B
6.	C		16.	A
7.	D		17.	C
8.	B		18.	B
9.	C		19.	A
10.	D		20.	D

21.	D
22.	D
23.	B
24.	B
25.	C

EXAMINATION SECTION
TEST 1

DIRECTIONS: In each of the following groups of sentences, one sentence is incorrect because it includes an error in grammar, usage, sentence structure, capitalization, diction, or punctuation. Indicate the INCORRECT sentence.

1. A. Under pressure, many school secretaries may become unnecessarily short and curt with visitors.
   B. She had not hardly opened the school office when she found a long line of mothers waiting to register their children.
   C. The discussion among the three secretaries helped to resolve the problem of responsibility for specific tasks.
   D. The principal said, "All of us are dependent on you for rapid and courteous telephone service."

1.____

2. A. "Why," she asked, "must I be responsible for training students helpers at the switchboard?"
   B. You must not doubt your ability to learn to prepare payroll reports.
   C. Learning to operate duplicating machines is an important part of a secretary's duties.
   D. I realize the values of promptness and accuracy in the office.

2.____

3. A. Never permit yourself to become so impersonal in your relationships that you lose your ability to get along with others.
   B. Please take this package to the teacher in room 304.
   C. Each of us has the task of arranging their own desks for quick and efficient work.
   D. I sent the pencils, paper, and books to the chairmen's offices.

3.____

4. A. Yesterday, the supplies were delivered; today, they must be distributed.
   B. The secretary sat down besides the new pupil to explain how the form was to be completed.
   C. Should you encounter an error made by a teacher on a report, please tell the teacher tactfully of the error.
   D. You may find it wise to proofread all items that you have typed before you remove them from the machine.

4.____

5. A. Did you understand the relay message to mean that all new secretaries must report for an orientation session?
   B. If you are asked to take dictation, make certain that you have the required items readily at hand.
   C. It is your responsibility to report any bomb threat to the ranking supervisor immediately.
   D. Irregardless of your previous instructions, you are not to permit students to go to the permanent record file.

5.____

6. A. She is one of those secretaries who is always accurate in her work.
   B. All of us agree that there should be some equitable distribution of office assignments.

6.____

115

C. As the school secretary picked up the telephone she heard a student shouting "Fire!" at the top of his voice.
D. You must be certain that the principal wishes to see a visitor before you usher the visitor into the principal's office.

7.
A. In so far as I am able, I shall attempt to serve all members of the community who enter the school office.
B. The school secretary who had typed the requisition had omitted the identifying number given in the supply list.
C. Her typing was as fast, if not faster than, any secretary he had ever had.
D. In order to complete the payroll, it may become necessary, on occasion, for the school secretary to remain beyond the regular school day.

7.____

8.
A. The school secretary with a firm knowledge of school accounts and records is an asset to any school office.
B. The accurate preparation of period attendance reports may enable the city to obtain its proper proportion of state funds.
C. Initiative on the part of the school secretary may result in improvement in the organization and administration of school routine.
D. "I seriously believe," she said, "that if we receive less than six helpers we cannot do the job."

8.____

9.
A. As the parent left the office, she said, "How can I ever repay you back for your kindness?"
B. Any money taken from the petty cash fund must be accounted for.
C. The requisitions had to be signed and dated before they could be mailed.
D. Needless to say, I urge you to be prompt and regular in attendance.

9.____

10.
A. Because all members of the office staff pitched in and helped, the huge task was completed in an extra ordinarily short period of time.
B. "If it cannot be completed by three o'clock, I am willing to stay overtime," she said.
C. Your typing has improved greatly both in accuracy and in speed.
D. Turning the page, the secretary's eye was attracted to the advertisement for a time-stamping device.

10.____

11.
A. The secretary said, "I do not mean to infer that I am displeased with this typewriter."
B. Relatively few of the children who came into the office had been given passes by their teachers.
C. The parent, who had been waiting for a long time before any attention was paid to her, vented her anger on the inconsiderate secretary.
D. The school secretary working in the general office very tactfully urged the teachers to lower their voices.

11.____

12.
A. The newly appointed member of the office staff was told that the assistant principal would tell her how to complete the report.
B. If you follow these suggestions, they will teach you self-control and to be tactful.
C. Observing the teacher's difficulty in understanding the pension statement, the school secretary offered to assist her.
D. She was most eager to learn the operation of the duplicating machine.

12.____

13. A. She took the reprimand very badly in that she assumed that it was an attack on her personally rather than on the nature of her work.
    B. By requesting the visitor to wait for a pass, she demonstrated that she was following the rules of the school.
    C. The notice on the bulletin board read: "Any discourtesy to our staff, if reported to the principal, will be greatly appreciated."
    D. May I have your permission to read the announcement over the public address system?

    13.____

14. A. You will undoubtedly become proficient as you gain experience.
    B. Have you been greatly effected in preparing the attendance reports by the transit strike?
    C. It is urgent that student monitors be sent to each of the classrooms with the message.
    D. Please keep an exact record of the date, time, and type of each fire drill that we conduct.

    14.____

15. A. If you take too much time during the mid-morning break, you place an extra burden on the secretaries who remain in the office.
    B. Please edit and proofread all notices before duplicating them.
    C. I do not anticipate any difficulty in developing the proper touch needed for operation of the electric type writer.
    D. In comparing the work done by the two school secretaries, I must admit that Miss Smith is the fastest typist.

    15.____

16. A. In the event that a teacher is absent from school, she is to call the school at 7:30 a.m. or as close to that time as possible.
    B. The notation on the "While You Were Out" slip indicated that Mr. Lane of the board of education had called.
    C. Decisions of these kinds may have to be made by you if no supervisor is available.
    D. What kind of information did the parent request?

    16.____

17. A. In answering the telephone, please give the name and borough of the school first.
    B. Why not try arranging the supplies neatly in your desk so that you can reach every item without difficulty?
    C. As she was preparing the list of names of students serving on the school newspaper staff, the secretary asked me how to list two editor-in-chiefs.
    D. Keep a list of printed forms that are in short supply so that we can order the forms we need.

    17.____

18. A. The secretary prepared a notice which was put in the mail boxes of all teachers, including yourself.
    B. Do not yield to the temptation to deal with a poorly dressed person in a way which is different from the way in which you treat others.
    C. You will find the envelope directly behind the file folder headed "Correspondence."
    D. May I ask you to double check the totals for each column so that you are certain that the addition is correct.

    18.____

19. A. Although the salesman was very persuasive, I refused to let him see the principal while the principal was in conference. 19.____
     B. Don't you think that it would be worth your while to improve the speed and accuracy of your typing?
     C. If the principal has left for the day, be sure to have the administrative assistant check the form before you duplicate it.
     D. We ordered the book before the special circular arrived describing the procedure to be followed.

20. A. The development of friction between co-workers is not inevitable. 20.____
     B. Do not be overly pessimistic about your ability to learn to prepare the period report correctly.
     C. Her manner with the children who come into the office is much too brusque and sharp, but I think that she is basically kind.
     D. The data is correct and, therefore, it may be incorporated into the report.

21. A. The best time to do work requiring full concentration is when the office is quiet. 21.____
     B. She inquired, "Are you going to hand in your report at 3:00 p.m.?"
     C. We should pay full attention to every kind of a written report.
     D. She learned that further practice had had a good effect on her ability to transcribe.

22. A. After brief training, she was ready to accept greater responsibility. 22.____
     B. According to my calendar, your examinations are due today for stencilling.
     C. Let's put aside this kind of work until later.
     D. Strict accuracy is a necessary requisite in record keeping.

23. A. Her desk was orderly, though piled high with folders; furthermore, her supplies were neatly arranged. 23.____
     B. She claims that our filing procedures need revision because they've become so boresome.
     C. "May I ask you, Miss Hawkins," said the principal's secretary, "to come in at once?"
     D. Oddly enough, he had forgotten to reset the school's clock for daylight saving time.

24. A. She had an almost hypnotic fascination for the rhythmical operation of the mimeograph machine. 24.____
     B. "Dr. Franklin, Professor Marlin, and Messrs. Clark, Havens, and Wilson will visit us today," wrote the principal in a memorandum.
     C. She quickly mastered the nomenclature of the supply catalogs.
     D. He informed all personnel not to furnish medicine to any pupil.

25. A. The pupil's account of his lateness is incredible, I will not give him a classroom pass. 25.____
     B. Her willingness to type was due to her desire to learn the forms.
     C. They scheduled their lunch hours in such a way that the switchboard could be covered constantly.
     D. She replenished her supply of clips, staples, bond paper, and pencils.

KEY (CORRECT ANSWERS)

1.	B	11.	A
2.	A	12.	B
3.	C	13.	C
4.	B	14.	B
5.	D	15.	D
6.	A	16.	B
7.	C	17.	C
8.	D	18.	A
9.	A	19.	D
10.	D	20.	D

21. C
22. D
23. B
24. A
25. A

TEST 2

DIRECTIONS: In each of the following groups of sentences, one sentence is incorrect because it includes an error in grammar, usage, sentence structure, capitalization, diction, or punctuation. Indicate the INCORRECT sentence.

1. A. They were thought to be we.
   B. The secretary whom we thought deserved the honor will receive a prize.
   C. The principal herself arranged the new library schedule.
   D. I am sorry to be unable to recommend a monitor for your office.

   1.____

2. A. Please lay the carbon paper on the proper shelf.
   B. The principal is expected to return inside of an hour.
   C. I seldom if ever make errors when I type letters.
   D. I feel confident that I am able to do this work accurately and neatly.

   2.____

3. A. To Mrs. Andersen have fallen the responsibilities of supply secretary.
   B. The secretary pointed out that all individuals under twenty-one years of age are legally considered minors.
   C. Mrs. Thompson, with her son and daughter, are going to the annual business show.
   D. There are fewer errors in this report than in the last report.

   3.____

4. A. One secretary referred to the project as "worthwhile and creative."
   B. I thought this typewriter was hers.
   C. A number of our secretarial staff is going on vacation soon.
   D. These typewriters are very sturdy: they are made from strong metal and unbreakable plastic.

   4.____

5. A. "I know," he said, "that you can finish this project today."
   B. I found Miss Jones the most cooperative of the two secretaries.
   C. My sister who works at Public School 73 lives in Manhattan.
   D. Our school secretary is always appropriately attired and well groomed.

   5.____

6. A. The letter has lain on the principal's desk all day, waiting for his signature.
   B. We believe that three-quarters of the work is done.
   C. She said, "Neither you nor I am responsible for that error."
   D. Let me speak to whomever is waiting for the assistant principal.

   6.____

7. A. How disappointing it was to hear him say, "Your bus has left!"
   B. It was a dark, dismal, dreary, December day.
   C. Do you know any alumnae of a women's college?
   D. It is imperative that you enunciate your words clearly when you use the telephone.

   7.____

8. A. "Will you have time," he inquired, "to prepare transcripts for our college-bound graduates?"
   B. You work more efficiently than her because you anticipate and avoid time-consuming trifles.

   8.____

C. Questions regarding procedure should be referred to a disinterested expert, should they not?
D. The chairmen of the health education, foreign language, mathematics, and English departments requested supply requisition forms.

9.
A. The instant the principal began to dictate, the bell rang, interrupting his train of thought.
B. This is one of those machines that are constantly breaking down.
C. She asked me whether I would remain a few additional minutes to check her report.
D. A well-organized schedule makes it possible to complete more work with less helpers.

9.____

10.
A. Teachers' letter boxes should not be filled in such a way as to create difficulty in removing individual 3" x 5" cards.
B. By being courteous, emotional outbursts can be avoided in discussions with irate parents.
C. Her transcribing was interrupted by the whirring, often much too loud, of the engines in the street.
D. In business letters, correct phrasing, as well as the avoidance of circumlocution, is a virtue.

10.____

11.
A. Listening intently to the heated discussion at the conference, Laura forgot to take notes; consequently, the minutes were incomplete.
B. If I were going to prepare the payroll report, I should begin as long in advance as possible.
C. She asked the student to bring the book to the principal.
D. The secretaries agreed among themselves that each would do a certain amount of correspondence.

11.____

12.
A. Ida had two tasks; namely, tabulating data and forwarding them to the assistant superintendent.
B. Your introduction to the members of the staff has been a pleasant experience, has it not.
C. "Between you and me, I can hardly tolerate that teacher anyhow," the angry mother confided.
D. Keeping the office windows fully closed may adversely affect secretaries' efficiency.

12.____

13.
A. From the tone of the letter, it was easy to imply that the writer was grateful.
B. We devised other means of communication since telephone extensions were nonexistent.
C. The preparation of circulars and attendance reports requires considerable care.
D. "Please direct me to room 205," said the visitor. "I have an appointment with Mr. Jones."

13.____

14.
A. An efficient school secretary in punctual, precise, and conscientious.
B. For a beginner, she gave a credulous performance on the piano.
C. I believe we had fewer pupils in the third grade last year.
D. Are you prepared to take dictation from the principal when he calls you?

14.____

15. A. I cannot help but congratulating you for the manner in which you handle the switch- 15.____
       board.
    B. This computer is broken; that hard drive is in need of repairs.
    C. Hurray! Here comes our school band!
    D. Having misplaced her key, the teacher borrowed one from the secretary.

16. A. Please deliver the message to either Miss Spring or her. 16.____
    B. I believe that ten dollars is not sufficient for the special type of paper you need.
    C. The most appreciated gift was the diaries you obtained for us.
    D. Our government found it necessary to discourage emigration to this country.

17. A. "What is the correct answer," she asked, "to question one on page 14 in the <u>Secre-</u> 17.____
       <u>tary's Manual</u>?"
    B. My sister Joan called on the phone to relay the important message.
    C. Please bring this material to the office of the custodian of the school.
    D. All secretaries should be aware of and familiar with the rules of indexing.

18. A. A majority of the members have promised to vote for Mr. Randolph. 18.____
    B. The work has been carefully laid out for you; you should have very little difficulty.
    C. His new book is as well written, though less exciting than, his previous book.
    D. Either you or she is the writer of this note and I doubt that it is she.

19. A. Will you please ship the books to us as soon as possible? 19.____
    B. A call was placed by Superintendent Donovan to the principal of the school.
    C. A strikeover is when a typist retypes a letter or number on top of the original
       incorrect one.
    D. The committee which the principal appointed consisted of three people: Mrs.
       Jones, a teacher; Robert; and Jane.

20. A. I was too greatly relieved to be able to say anything. 20.____
    B. These insignia date back to ancient Roman times.
    C. We observed a strange phenomenon; the house seemed to sway in the wind
       and to tremble like a leaf.
    D. It would be much more preferable if you were no longer seen in his company.

21. A. Please send me this data at your earliest convenience. 21.____
    B. The loss of their material proved a severe handicap.
    C. My principal objection to this plan is that it is impracticable.
    D. The doll has lain in the rain all evening.

22. A. I had expected to see my brother. 22.____
    B. He expected to have seen his brother.
    C. I hoped to see you do better.
    D. It was his duty to assist our friend.

23. A. The reason why I am writing to you is that I wish to avoid further misunderstanding. 23.____
    B. These kind of arguments always cause hard feelings.
    C. Regardless of your decision, I shall have to go.
    D. I have only twenty pupils in this class.

24. A. Which is the youngest of the two sisters? 24.____
    B. I am determined to finish the work before Saturday.
    C. It is difficult to see why the problems are not correctly solved.
    D. I have never met a more interesting person.

25. A. Located on a mountainside with a babbling brook beside the door, it was a dream palace. 25.____
    B. Blessed are they that have not seen and yet have believed.
    C. The customs in that part of the country are much different than I expected.
    D. Politics, even in towns of small population, has always attracted ambitious young lawyers.

KEY (CORRECT ANSWERS)

1.	B	11.	C
2.	B	12.	B
3.	C	13.	A
4.	C	14.	B
5.	B	15.	A
6.	D	16.	D
7.	B	17.	C
8.	B	18.	C
9.	D	19.	C
10.	B	20.	D

21. A
22. B
23. B
24. A
25. C

TEST 3

DIRECTIONS: In each of the following groups of sentences, one of the four sentences is faulty in grammar, punctuation, or capitalization. Select the INCORRECT sentence in each case.

1. A. If you had stood at home and done your homework, you would not have failed in arithmetic.
    B. Her affected manner annoyed every member of the audience.
    C. How will the new law affect our income taxes?
    D. The plants were not affected by the long, cold winter, but they succumbed to the drought of summer.

1.____

2. A. He is one of the most able men who have been in the Senate.
    B. It is he who is to blame for the lamentable mistake.
    C. Haven't you a helpful suggestion to make at this time?
    D. The money was robbed from the blind man's cup.

2.____

3. A. The amount of children in this school is steadily increasing.
    B. After taking an apple from the table, she went out to play.
    C. He borrowed a dollar from me.
    D. I had hoped my brother would arrive before me.

3.____

4. A. Whom do you think I hear from every week?
    B. Who do you think is the right man for the job?
    C. Who do you think I found in the room?
    D. He is the man whom we considered a good candidate for the presidency.

4.____

5. A. Quietly the puppy laid down before the fireplace.
    B. You have made your bed; now lie in it.
    C. I was badly sunburned because I had lain too long in the sun.
    D. I laid the doll on the bed and left the room.

5.____

6. A. Sailing down the bay was a thrilling experience for me.
    B. He was not consulted about your joining the club.
    C. This story is different than the one I told you yesterday.
    D. There is no doubt about his being the best player.

6.____

7. A. He maintains there is but one road to world peace.
    B. It is common knowledge that a child sees much he is not supposed to see.
    C. Much of the bitterness might have been avoided if arbitration had been resorted to earlier in the meeting.
    D. The man decided it would be advisable to marry a girl somewhat younger than him.

7.____

8. A. We have received complaints to the effect that the school's clocks are not synchronized.
    B. My telephone is busier than the others, and so why don't they help me out?
    C. If you had mislaid Mr. Harris' file, would you not have informed the principal immediately?
    D. Please distribute these newly-arrived pension booklets among all the teachers.

8.____

9. A. One should partake in the orientation discussion and heed the council of one's co-workers.
    B. A general circular was drawn up to correct misunderstanding created by the poorly-worded notice on the bulletin board.
    C. We divide teachers' checks into two alphabetized groups for equitable distribution.
    D. Her initiative has led to a streamlining of cumbersome routines.

10. A. We have just begun to assemble the figures for the period attendance report.
    B. She reports promptly to her assigned station during fire drills.
    C. The person who telephoned insisted on speaking directly to the principal.
    D. "Have you decided, he asked," to prepare the calendar for the remainder of the term?"

11. A. Give this message to whomever you think is a reliable monitor.
    B. You are not allowed to send pupils out of the building without the principal's permission.
    C. The postman placed the mail, tied with strong cord, in front of the time clock.
    D. We mailed notices to no fewer than 280 parents.

12. A. She is reluctantly seeking a transfer because she is going to move.
    B. Miss Wilson, when did we conduct our last shelter area drill?
    C. Since no monitor was available, Miss Foster delivered the message herself.
    D. I'd like an appointment to a school in the east side.

13. A. The information acquired by the school secretary who types observation reports must remain confidential.
    B. You should be impartial to all without sacrificing your friendly approach.
    C. The mail was sorted without they're having to take time from preparing the report.
    D. Your desk will have to be moved while the repairman is working on the ceiling.

14. A. She sent a copy of "How Good Are Our Schools?" reprinted from American Education.
    B. It is long past the time the bell should have rang.
    C. She counted twenty one-dollar bills in the petty cash reserve.
    D. The reason he returned the stencil was that he had found too many errors.

15. A. Dr. Smith, professor of American literature, was the principal speaker.
    B. "Which one of you," asked the principal, "prepared this report?"
    C. There are distinct differences between shorthand, type writing and filing.
    D. I intend to devote the balance of the day to the preparation of the reports.

16. A. Either the librarian or the pupils are wrong.
    B. "Who," asked the principal, "said, 'Correct practice makes perfect'?"
    C. We have the supplies in this cabinet: letterheads, onionskin paper, envelopes, carbon paper, and pencils.
    D. Walking through the corridor, a fire extinguisher came into view.

17. A. The two secretaries entered the lunch room and sat besides us.
    B. The secretary's success is due to her conscientiousness.
    C. If you find the papers, please let me know about it; but you are certain to have to hunt for them.
    D. I am able to change a typewriter ribbon and to make minor typewriter adjustments.

17.____

18. A. The choice of a typewriter is difficult, there are many excellent ones on the market today.
    B. We have sold an unusually large number of pens in the school store.
    C. Our principal constantly emphasizes punctuality and excellent attendance.
    D. What do you think the effect of the decision will be?

18.____

19. A. The last carton of the new envelopes have just been opened.
    B. The secretary inquired, "Did you hear him ask, 'Who are you?'"
    C. Instead of a 2 and a 7 she had typed two 4's.
    D. She might — and according to plans, should — have completed the project.

19.____

20. A. This here typewriter is the one that is not working well.
    B. I believe that it's time for the bell to ring.
    C. Mr. Clark called us, Evelyn and me, into his office.
    D. Jean and I can distribute the mail before noon.

20.____

21. A. Many a clerk and stenographer has become an efficient school secretary.
    B. The data was assembled by three of our secretaries who served on the committee.
    C. I don't know, Mr. Thompson, where your secretary is.
    D. She was typing the letters accurately and rapidly, of course.

21.____

22. A. I do not say exactly that these stories are not true; I only say that I do not believe them.
    B. My old fountain pen, which never leaked or clogged, is broken and I can use it no further.
    C. Compare the quality of our papers with any other papers in the same price range. There is just no comparison.
    D. Today's news, in the words of a famous Frenchman, is in yesterday's newspaper; tomorrow's, in today's.

22.____

23. A. She objected to his reading comics and told him to put it away.
    B. The patient said that the doctor had ordered him to lie down every day after dinner for two hours and that he had, in fact, lain down for more than three hours.
    C. We are likely to run out of money before our vacation is over, and we shall have to borrow some from our friends.
    D. We are confident that you will appoint whomever is best suited for the position.

23.____

24. A. "Age is like love: it cannot be hid." —Thomas Dekker
    B. The question Mary refused to answer was: Did you see Mr. Clark actually leave the building?
    C. This information, namely, that we are going out of business, is accurate.
    D. The Joneses' house is in excellent condition because Mr. and Mrs. Jones take such good care of it.

24.____

25. A. He, not she, is the one to go because he is better prepared than her; thus he can do the job as well as she and we can be sure that it will be done properly.
    B. She had no sooner entered the office and begun to type than the bell announced the first coffee break of the day.
    C. While there has been considerable scholarly interest in the subject, there have been hardly any scientific experiments of any value in the field.
    D. I played the song "Getting To Know You" from the record "The King and I."

25.____

KEY (CORRECT ANSWERS)

1. A
2. D
3. A
4. C
5. A

6. C
7. D
8. B
9. A
10. C

11. A
12. D
13. C
14. B
15. D

16. D
17. A
18. A
19. A
20. A

21. B
22. C
23. D
24. B
25. A

PREPARING WRITTEN MATERIALS
EXAMINATION SECTION
TEST 1

DIRECTIONS: Each question or incomplete statement is followed by several suggested answers or completions. Select the one that BEST answers the question or completes the statement. *PRINT THE LETTER OF THE CORRECT ANSWER IN THE SPACE AT THE RIGHT.*

Questions 1-21.

DIRECTIONS: In each of the following sentences, which were taken from students' transcripts, there may be an error. Indicate the appropriate correction in the space at the right. If the sentence is correct as is, indicate this choice. Unnecessary changes will be considered incorrect.

1. In that building there seemed to be representatives of Teachers College, the Veterans Bureau, and the Businessmen's Association.
    A. Teacher's College
    B. Veterans' Bureau
    C. Businessmens Association
    D. Correct as is

    1.____

2. In his travels, he visited St. Paul, San Francisco, Springfield, Ohio, and Washington, D.C.
    A. Ohio and
    B. Saint Paul
    C. Washington, D.C.
    D. Correct as is

    2.____

3. As a result of their purchasing a controlling interest in the syndicate, it was well-known that the Bureau of Labor Statistics' calculations would be unimportant.
    A. of them purchasing
    B. well known
    C. Statistics
    D. Correct as is

    3.____

4. Walter Scott, Jr.'s, attempt to emulate his father's success was doomed to failure.
    A. Junior's,
    B. Scott's, Jr.
    C. Scott, Jr.'s attempt
    D. Correct as is

    4.____

5. About B.C. 250 the Romans invaded Great Britain, and remains of their highly developed civilization can still be seen.
    A. 250 B.C.
    B. Britain and
    C. highly-developed
    D. Correct as is

    5.____

6. The two boss's sons visited the children's department.
    A. bosses
    B. bosses'
    C. childrens'
    D. Correct as is

    6.____

7. Miss Amex not only approved the report, but also decided that it needed no revision.
   A. report; but   B. report but   C. report. But   D. Correct as is

8. Here's brain food in a jiffy—economical, too!
   A. economical too!
   B. "brain food"
   C. jiffy-economical
   D. Correct as is

9. She said, "He likes the "Gatsby Look" very much."
   A. said "He
   B. "he
   C. 'Gatsby Look'
   D. Correct as is

10. We anticipate that we will be able to visit them briefly in Los Angeles on Wednesday after a five day visit.
    A. Wednes-   B. 5 day   C. five-day   D. Correct as is

11. She passed all her tests, and, she now has a good position.
    A. tests, and she
    B. past
    C. tests;
    D. Correct as is

12. The billing clerk said, "I will send the bill today"; however, that was a week ago, and it hasn't arrived yet!
    A. today;"   B. today,"   C. ago and   D. Correct as is

13. "She types at more-than-average speed," Miss Smith said, "but I feel that it is a result of marvelous concentration and self control on her part."
    A. more than average
    B. "But
    C. self-control
    D. Correct as is

14. The state of Alaska, the largest state in the union, is also the northernmost state.
    A. Union
    B. Northernmost State
    C. State of Alaska
    D. Correct as is

15. The memoirs of Ex-President Nixon, according to figures, sold more copies than Six Crises, the book he wrote in the '60s.
    A. Six Crises
    B. ex-President
    C. 60s
    D. Correct as is

16. "There are three principal elements, determining the hazard of buildings: the contents hazard, the fire resistance of the structure, and the character of the interior finish," concluded the speaker.
    The one of the following statements that is MOST acceptable is that, in the above passage,
    A. the comma following the word *elements* is incorrect
    B. the colon following the word *buildings* is incorrect
    C. the comma following the word *finish* is incorrect
    D. there is no error in the punctuation of the sentence

17. He spoke on his favorite topic, "Why We Will Win." (How could I stop him?) 17._____
   A. Win". B. him?). C. him)? C. Correct as is

18. "All any insurance policy is, is a contract for services," said my insurance 18._____
   agent, Mr. Newton.
   A. Insurance Policy B. Insurance Agent
   C. policy is is a D. Correct as is

19. Inasmuch as the price list has now been up dated, we should sent it to the 19._____
   printer.
   A. In as much B. updated
   C. pricelist D. Correct as is

20. We feel that "Our know-how" is responsible for the improvement in technical 20._____
   developments.
   A. "our B. know how C. that, D. Correct as is

21. Did Cortez conquer the Incas? the Aztecs? the South American Indians? 21._____
   A. Incas, the Aztecs, the South American Indians?
   B. Incas; the Aztecs; the South American Indians?
   C. south American Indians?
   D. Correct as is

22. Which one of the following forms for the typed name of the dictator in the closing 22._____
   lines of a letter is generally MOST acceptable in the United States?
   A. (Dr.) James F. Farley B. Dr. James F. Farley
   C. Me. James J. Farley, Ph.D. D. James F. Farley

23. The plural of 23._____
   A. turkey is turkies B. cargo is cargoes
   C. bankruptcy is bankruptcys D. son-in-law is son-in-laws

24. The abbreviation viz. means MOST NEARLY 24._____
   A. namely B. for example
   C. the following D. see

25. In the sentence, *A man in a light-gray suit waited thirty-five minutes in the* 25._____
   ante-room for the all-important document, the word IMPROPERLY hyphenated
   is
   A. light-gray B. thirty-five C. ante-room D. all-important

KEY (CORRECT ANSWERS)

1.	D	11.	A
2.	C	12.	D
3.	B	13.	D
4.	D	14.	A
5.	A	15.	B
6.	B	16.	A
7.	B	17.	D
8.	D	18.	D
9.	C	19.	B
10.	C	20.	A

21. D
22. D
23. B
24. A
25. C

TEST 2

DIRECTIONS: Each question or incomplete statement is followed by several suggested answers or completions. Select the one that BEST answers the question or completes the statement. *PRINT THE LETTER OF THE CORRECT ANSWER IN THE SPACE AT THE RIGHT.*

Questions 1-10.

DIRECTIONS: In each of the following groups of four sentences, one sentence contains an error in sentence structure, grammar, usage, diction, or punctuation. Indicate the INCORRECT sentence.

1. A. The lecture finished, the audience began asking questions.
   B. Any man who could accomplish that task the world would regard as a hero.
   C. Our respect and admiration are mutual.
   D. George did like his mother told him, despite the importunities of his playmates.

2. A. I cannot but help admiring you for your dedication to your job.
   B. Because they had insisted upon showing us films of their travels, we have lost many friends whom we once cherished.
   C. I am constrained to admit that your remarks made me feel bad.
   D. My brother having been notified of his acceptance by the university of his choice, my father immediately made plans for a vacation.

3. A. In no other country is freedom of speech and assembly so jealously guarded.
   B. Being a beatnik, he felt that it would be a betrayal of his cause to wear shoes and socks at the same time.
   C. Riding over the Brooklyn Bridge gave us an opportunity to see the Manhattan skyline.
   D. In 1961, flaunting SEATO, the North Vietnamese crossed the line of demarcation.

4. A. I have enjoyed the study of the Spanish language not only because of its beauty and the opportunity it offers to understand the Hispanic culture but also to make use of it in the business associations I have in South America.
   B. The opinions he expressed were decidedly different from those he had held in his youth.
   C. Had he actually studied, he certainly would have passed.
   D. A supervisor should be patient, tactful, and firm.

5. A. At this point we were faced with only three alternatives: to push on, to remain where we were, or to return to the village.
   B. We had no choice but to forgive so venial a sin.
   C. In their new picture, the Warners are flouting tradition.
   D. Photographs taken revealed that 2.5 square miles had been burned.

6. A. He asked whether he might write to his friends.
    B. There are many problems which must be solved before we can be assured of world peace.
    C. Each person with whom I talked expressed his opinion freely.
    D. Holding on to my saddle with all my strength the horse galloped down the road at a terrifying pace.

7. A. After graduating high school, he obtained a position as a runner in Wall Street.
    B. Last night, in a radio address, the President urged us to subscribe to the Red Cross.
    C. In the evening, light spring rain cooled the streets.
    D. "Un-American" is a word which has been used even by those whose sympathies may well have been pro-Nazi.

8. A. It is hard to conceive of their not doing good work.
    B. Who won—you or I?
    C. He having read the speech caused much comment.
    D. Their finishing the work proves that it can be done.

9. A. Our course of study should not be different now than it was five years ago.
    B. I cannot deny myself the pleasure of publicly thanking the mayor for his actions.
    C. The article on "Morale" has appeared in the Times Literary Supplement.
    D. He died of tuberculosis contracted during service with the Allied Forces.

10. A. If it wasn't for a lucky accident, he would still be an office-clerk.
    B. It is evident that teachers need help.
    C. Rolls of postage stamps may be bought at stationery stores.
    D. Addressing machines are used by firms that publish magazines.

11. The one of the following sentences which contains NO error in usage is:
    A. After the robbers left, the proprietor stood tied in his chair for about two hours before help arrived.
    B. In the cellar I found the watchmans' hat and coat.
    C. The persons living in adjacent apartments stated that they had heard no unusual noises.
    D. Neither a knife or any firearms were found in the room.

12. The one of the following sentences which contains NO error in usage is:
    A. The policeman lay a firm hand on the suspect's shoulder.
    B. It is true that neither strength nor agility are the most important requirement for a good patrolman.
    C. Good citizens constantly strive to do more than merely comply the restraints imposed by society.
    D. Twenty years is considered a severe sentence for a felony.

13. Select the sentence containing an adverbial objective. 13._____
    A. Concepts can only acquire content when they are connected, however indirectly, with sensible experience.
    B. The cloth was several shades too light to match the skirt which she had discarded.
    C. The Gargantuan Hall of Commons became a tri-daily horror to Kurt, because two youths discerned that he had a beard and courageously told the world about it.
    D. Brooding morbidly over the event, Elsie found herself incapable of engaging in normal activity.

14. Select the sentence containing a verb in the subjunctive mood. 14._____
    A. Had he known of the new experiments with penicillin dust for the cure of colds, he might have been tempted to try them in his own office.
    B. I should be very much honored by your visit.
    C. Though he has one of the highest intelligence quotients in his group, he seems far below the average in actual achievement.
    D. Long had I known that he would be the man finally selected for such signal honors.

15. Select the sentence containing one (or more) passive perfect participle(s). 15._____
    A. Having been apprised of the consequences of his refusal to answer, the witness finally revealed the source of his information.
    B. To have been placed in such an uncomfortable position was perhaps unfair to a journalist of his reputation.
    C. When deprived of special immunity he had, of course, no alternative but to speak.
    D. Having been obdurate until now, he was reluctant to surrender under this final pressure exerted upon him.

16. Select the sentence containing a predicate nominative. 16._____
    A. His dying wish, which he expressed almost with his last breath, was to see that justice was done toward his estranged wife.
    B. So long as we continue to elect our officials in truly democratic fashion, we shall have the power to preserve our liberties.
    C. We could do nothing, at this juncture, but walk the five miles back to camp.
    D. There was the spaniel, wet and cold and miserable, waiting silently at the door.

17. Select the sentence containing exactly TWO adverbs. 17._____
    A. The gentlemen advanced with exasperating deliberateness, while his lonely partner waited.
    B. If you are well, will you come early?
    C. I think you have guessed right, though you were rather slow, I must say.
    D. The last hundred years have seen more change than a thousand years of the Roman Empire, than a hundred thousand years of the stone age.

Questions 18-24.

DIRECTIONS: Select the choice describing the error in the sentence.

18. If us seniors do not support school functions, who will?
    A. Unnecessary shift in tense
    B. Incomplete sentence
    C. Improper case of pronoun
    D. Lack of parallelism

19. The principal has issued regulations which, in my opinion, I think are too harsh.
    A. Incorrect punctuation
    B. Faulty sentence structure
    C. Misspelling
    D. Redundant expression

20. The freshmens' and sophomores' performances equaled those of the juniors and seniors.
    A. Ambiguous reference
    B. Incorrect placement of punctuation
    C. Misspelling of past tense
    D. Incomplete comparison

21. Each of them, Anne and her, is an outstanding pianist I can't tell you which one is best.
    A. Lack of agreement
    B. Improper degree of comparison
    C. Incorrect case of pronoun
    D. Run-on sentence

22. She wears clothes that are more expensive than my other friends.
    A. Misuse of *than*
    B. Incorrect relative pronoun
    C. Shift in tense
    D. Faulty comparison

23. At the very end of the story it implies that the children's father died tragically.
    A. Misuse of *implies*
    B. Indefinite use of pronoun
    C. Incorrect spelling
    D. Incorrect possessive

24. At the end of the game both of us, John and me, couldn't scarcely walk because we were so tired.
    A. Incorrect punctuation
    B. Run-on sentence
    C. Incorrect case of pronoun
    D. Double negative

Questions 25-30.

DIRECTIONS: Questions 25 through 30 consist of a sentence lacking certain needed punctuation. Pick as your answer the description of punctuation which will CORRECTLY complete the sentence.

25. If you take the time to keep up your daily correspondence you will no doubt be most efficient.
    A. Comma only after *doubt*
    B. Comma only after *correspondence*
    C. Commas after *correspondence*, *will*, and *be*
    D. Commas after *if*, *correspondence*, and *will*

26. Because he did not send the application soon enough he did not receive the up to date copy of the book. 26.____
    A. Commas after *application* and *enough*, and quotation marks before *up* and after *date*
    B. Commas after *application* and *enough*, and hyphens between *to* and *date*
    C. Comma after *enough*, and hyphens between *up* and *to* and between *to* and *date*
    D. Comma after *application*, and quotation marks before *up* and after *date*

27. The coordinator requested from the department the following items a letter each week summarizing progress personal forms and completed applications for tests. 27.____
    A. Commas after *items* and *completed*
    B. Semi-colon after *items* and *progress*, comma after *forms*
    C. Colon after *items*, commas after *progress* and *forms*
    D. Colon after *items*, commas after *forms* and *applications*

28. The supervisor asked Who will attend the conference next month. 28.____
    A. Comma after *asked*, period after *month*
    B. Period after *asked*, question mark after *month*
    C. Comma after *asked*, quotation marks before *Who*, quotation marks after *month*, and question mark after the quotation marks
    D. Comma after *asked*, quotation marks before *Who*, question mark after *month*, and quotation marks after the question mark

29. When the statistics are collected, we will forward the results to you as soon as possible. 29.____
    A. Comma after *you*
    B. Commas after *forward* and *you*
    C. Commas after *collected*, *results* and *you*
    D. Comma after *collected*

30. The ecology of our environment is concerned with mans pollution of the atmosphere. 30.____
    A. Comma after *ecology*
    B. Apostrophe after *n* and before *s* in *mans*
    C. Commas after *ecology* and *environment*
    D. Apostrophe after *s* in *mans*

KEY (CORRECT ANSWERS)

1.	D	11.	C	21.	B
2.	A	12.	D	22.	D
3.	D	13.	B	23.	B
4.	A	14.	A	24.	D
5.	B	15.	A	25.	B
6.	D	16.	A	26.	C
7.	A	17.	C	27.	C
8.	C	18.	C	28.	D
9.	A	19.	D	29.	D
10.	A	20.	B	30.	B

TEST 3

DIRECTIONS: Each question or incomplete statement is followed by several suggested answers or completions. Select the one that BEST answers the question or completes the statement. *PRINT THE LETTER OF THE CORRECT ANSWER IN THE SPACE AT THE RIGHT.*

Questions 1-6.

DIRECTIONS: From the four choices offered in Questions 1 through 6, select the one which is INCORRECT.

1.
   A. Before we try to extricate ourselves from this struggle in which we are now engaged in, we must be sure that we are not severing ties of honor and duty.
   B. Besides being an outstanding student, he is also a leader in school government and a trophy-winner in school sports.
   C. If the framers of the Constitution were to return to life for a day, their opinion of our amendments would be interesting.
   D. Since there are three m's in the word, it is frequently misspelled.

   1.____

2.
   A. It was a college with an excellance beyond question.
   B. The coach will accompany the winners, whomever they may be.
   C. The dean, together with some other faculty members, is planning a conference.
   D. The jury are arguing among themselves.

   2.____

3.
   A. This box is less nearly square than that one.
   B. Wagner is many persons' choice as the world's greatest composer.
   C. The habits of Copperheads are different from Diamond Backs.
   D. The teacher maintains that the child was insolent.

   3.____

4.
   A. There was a time when the Far North was unknown territory. Now American soldiers manning radar stations there wave to Boeing jet planes zooming by overhead.
   B. Exodus, the psalms, and Deuteronomy are all books of the Old Testament.
   C. Linda identified her china dishes by marking their bottoms with india ink.
   D. Harry S. Truman, former president of the United States, served as a captain in the American army during World War I.

   4.____

5.
   A. The sequel of their marriage was a divorce.
   B. We bought our car secondhand.
   C. His whereabouts is unknown.
   D. Jones offered to use his own car, providing the company would pay for gasoline, oil, and repairs,

   5.____

6. A. I read Golding's "Lord of the Flies".
    B. The orator at the civil rights rally thrilled the audience when he said, "I quote Robert Burns's line, 'A man's a man for a' that."
    C. The phrase "producer to consumer" is commonly used by market analysts.
    D. The lawyer shouted, "Is not this evidence illegal?"

Questions 7-9.

DIRECTIONS: In answering Questions 7 through 9, mark the letter A if faulty because of incorrect grammar, mark the letter B if faulty because of incorrect punctuation, mark the letter C if correct.

7. Mr. Brown our accountant, will audit the accounts next week.

8. Give the assignment to whomever is able to do it most efficiently.

9. The supervisor expected either your or I to file these reports.

Questions 10-14.

DIRECTIONS: In each of the following groups of four sentences, one sentence contains an error in sentence structure, grammar, usage, diction, or punctuation. Indicate the INCORRECT sentence.

10. A. The agent asked, "Did you say, 'Never again?'"
    B. Kindly let me know whether you can visit us on the 17th.
    C. "I cannot accept that!" he exploded. "Please show me something else.
    D. Ed, will you please lend me your grass shears for an hour or so.

11. A. Recalcitrant though he may have been, Alexander was willfully destructive.
    B. Everybody should look out for himself.
    C. John is one of those students who usually spends most of his time in the principal's office.
    D. She seems to feel that what is theirs is hers.

12. A. Be he ever so much in the wrong, I'll support the man while deploring his actions.
    B. The schools' lack of interest in consumer education is shortsighted.
    C. I think that Fitzgerald's finest stanza is one which includes the reference to youth's "sweet-scented manuscript.
    D. I never would agree to Anderson having full control of the company's policies.

13. A. We had to walk about five miles before finding a gas station.
    B. The willful sending of a false alarm has, and may, result in homicide.
    C. Please bring that book to me at once.
    D. Neither my sister nor I am interested in bowling.

14. A. He is one of the very few football players who doesn't wear a helmet with a face guard. 14.____
    B. But three volunteers appeared at the recruiting office.
    C. Such consideration as you can give us will be appreciated.
    D. When I left them, the group were disagreeing about the proposed legislation.

Question 15.

DIRECTIONS: Question 15 contains two sentences concerning criminal law. The sentences could contain errors in English grammar or usage. A sentence does not contain an error simply because it could be written in a different manner. In answering this question, choose answer
A. if only sentence I is correct
B. if only sentence II is correct
C. if both sentences are correct
D. if neither sentence is correct

15. I. The use of fire or explosives to destroy tangible property is proscribed by the criminal mischief provisions of the Revised Penal Law. 15.____
    II. The defendant's taking of a taxicab for the immediate purpose of affecting his escape did not constitute grand larceny.

KEY (CORRECT ANSWERS)

1.	A	6.	A	11.	C
2.	B	7.	B	12.	D
3.	C	8.	A	13.	B
4.	B	9.	A	14.	A
5.	D	10	A	15.	A

PREPARING WRITTEN MATERIAL

PARAGRAPH REARRANGEMENT
COMMENTARY

The sentences that follow are in scrambled order. You are to rearrange them in proper order and indicate the letter choice containing the correct answer at the space at the right.

Each group of sentences in this section is actually a paragraph presented in scrambled order. Each sentence in the group has a place in that paragraph; no sentence is to be left out. You are to read each group of sentences and decide upon the best order in which to put the sentences so as to form a well-organized paragraph.

The questions in this section measure the ability to solve a problem when all the facts relevant to its solution are not given.

More specifically, certain positions of responsibility and authority require the employee to discover connection between events sometimes, apparently, unrelated. In order to do this, the employee will find it necessary to correctly infer that unspecified events have probably occurred or are likely to occur. This ability becomes especially important when action must be taken on incomplete information.

Accordingly, these questions require competitors to choose among several suggested alternatives, each of which presents a different sequential arrangement of the events. Competitors must choose the MOST logical of the suggested sequences.

In order to do so, they may be required to draw on general knowledge to infer missing concepts or events that are essential to sequencing the given events. Competitors should be careful to infer only what is essential to the sequence. The plausibility of the wrong alternatives will always require the inclusion of unlikely events or of additional chains of events which are NOT essential to sequencing the given events.

It's very important to remember that you are looking for the best of the four possible choices, and that the best choice of all may not even be one of the answers you're given to choose from.

There is no one right way to solve these problems. Many people have found it helpful to first write out the order of the sentences, as they would have arranged them, on their scrap paper before looking at the possible answers. If their optimum answer is there, this can save them some time. If it isn't, this method can still give insight into solving the problem. Others find it most helpful to just go through each of the possible choices, contrasting each as they go along. You should use whatever method feels comfortable and works for you.

While most of these types of questions are not that difficult, we've added a higher percentage of the difficult type, just to give you more practice. Usually there are only one or two questions on this section that contain such subtle distinctions that you're unable to answer confidently. And you then may find yourself stuck deciding between two possible choices, neither of which you're sure about.

EXAMINATION SECTION

TEST 1

DIRECTIONS: The sentences that follow are in scrambled order. You are to rearrange them in proper order and indicate the letter choice containing the correct answer. *PRINT THE LETTER OF THE CORRECT ANSWER IN THE SPACE AT THE RIGHT.*

1. Below are four statements labeled W, X, Y and Z.
   W. He was a strict and fanatic drillmaster.
   X. The word is always used in a derogatory sense and generally shows resentment and anger on the part of the user.
   Y. It is from the name of this Frenchman that we derive our English word, martinet.
   Z. Jean Martinet was the Inspector-General of Infantry during the reign of King Louis XIV.
   The PROPER order in which these sentences should be placed in a paragraph is:
     A. X, Z, W, Y   B. X, Z, Y, W   C. Z, W, Y, X   D. Z, Y, W, X

   1.____

2. In the following paragraph, the sentences, which are numbered, have been jumbled.
   I. Since then it has undergone changes.
   II. It was incorporated in 1955 under the laws of the State of New York.
   III. Its primary purposes, a cleaner city, has, however, remained the same.
   IV. The Citizens Committee works in cooperation with the Mayor's Inter-departmental Committee for a Clean City.
   The order in which these sentences should be arranged to form a well-organized paragraph is:
     A. II, IV, I, III   B. III, IV, I, II   C. IV, II, I, III   D. IV, III, II, I

   2.____

   3.____

Questions 3-5.

DIRECTIONS: The sentences listed below are part of a meaningful paragraph but they are not given in their proper order. You are to decide what would be the BEST order in which to put the sentences so as to form a well-organized paragraph. Each sentence has a place in the paragraph; there are no extra sentences. You are then to answer Questions 3 through 5 inclusive on the basis of your rearrangements of these scrambled sentences into a properly organized paragraph.

In 1887 some insurance companies organized an Inspection Department to advise their clients on all phases of fire prevention and protection. Probably this has been due to the smaller annual fire losses in Great Britain than in the United States. It tests various fire prevention devices and appliances and determines manufacturing hazards and their safeguards. Fire research began earlier in the United States and is more advanced than in Great Britain. Later they established a laboratory specializing in electrical, mechanical, hydraulic, and chemical fields.

3. When the five sentences are arranged in proper order, the paragraph starts with the sentence which begins
    A. "In 1887…"
    B. "Probably this…"
    C. "It tests…"
    D. "Fire research…"
    E. "Later they…"

4. In the last sentence listed above, "they" refers to
    A. the insurance companies
    B. the United States and Great Britain
    C. the Inspection Department
    D. clients
    E. technicians

5. When the above paragraph is properly arranged, it ends with the words
    A. "…and protection."
    B. "…the United States."
    C. "…their safeguards."
    D. "…in Great Britain."
    E. "…chemical fields."

KEY (CORRECT ANSWERS)

1. C
2. C
3. D
4. A
5. C

TEST 2

DIRECTIONS: In each of the questions numbered I through V, several sentences are given. For each question, choose as your answer the group of number that represents the MOST logical order of these sentences if they were arranged in paragraph form. *PRINT THE LETTER OF THE CORRECT ANSWER IN THE SPACE AT THE RIGHT.*

1.
   I. It is established when one shows that the landlord has prevented the tenant's enjoyment of his interest in the property leased.
   II. Constructive eviction is the result of a breach of the covenant of quiet enjoyment implied in all leases.
   III. In some parts of the United States, it is not complete until the tenant vacates within a reasonable time.
   IV. Generally, the acts must be of such serious and permanent character as to deny the tenant the enjoyment of his possessing rights.
   V. In this event, upon abandonment of the premises, the tenant's liability for that ceases.
   The CORRECT answer is:
   A. II, I, IV, III, V
   B. V, II, III, I, IV
   C. IV, III, I, II, V
   D. I, III, V, IV, II

   1.____

2.
   I. The powerlessness before private and public authorities that is the typical experience of the slum tenant is reminiscent of the situation of blue-collar workers all through the nineteenth century.
   II. Similarly, in recent years, this chapter of history has been reopened by anti-poverty groups which have attempted to organize slum tenants to enable them to bargain collectively with their landlords about the conditions of their tenancies.
   III. It is familiar history that many of the worker remedied their condition by joining together and presenting their demands collectively.
   IV. Like the workers, tenants are forced by the conditions of modern life into substantial dependence on these who possess great political aid and economic power.
   V. What's more, the very fact of dependence coupled with an absence of education and self-confidence makes them hesitant and unable to stand up for what they need from those in power.
   The CORRECT answer is:
   A. V, IV, I, II, III
   B. II, III, I, V, IV
   C. III, I, V, IV, II
   D. I, IV, V, III, II

   2.____

3.
   I. A railroad, for example, when not acting as a common carrier may contract away responsibility for its own negligence.
   II. As to a landlord, however, no decision has been found relating to the legal effect of a clause shifting the statutory duty of repair to the tenant.
   III. The courts have not passed on the validity of clauses relieving the landlord of this duty and liability.
   IV. They have, however, upheld the validity of exculpatory clauses in other types of contracts.

   3.____

147

V. Housing regulations impose a duty upon the landlord to maintain leased premises in safe condition.
VI. As another example, a bailee may limit his liability except for gross negligence, willful acts, or fraud.

The CORRECT answer is:
A. II, I, VI, IV, III, V
B. I, III, IV, V, VI, II
C. III, V, I, IV, II, VI
D. V, III, IV, I, VI, II

4. I. Since there are only samples in the building, retail or consumer sales are generally eschewed by mart occupants, and in some instances, rigid controls are maintained to limit entrance to the mart only to those persons engaged in retailing.
II. Since World War I, in many larger cities, there has developed a new type of property, called the mart building.
III. It can, therefore, be used by wholesalers and jobbers for the display of sample merchandise.
IV. This type of building is most frequently a multi-storied, finished interior property which is a cross between a retail arcade and a loft building.
V. This limitation enables the mart occupants to ship the orders from another location after the retailer or dealer makes his selection from the samples.

The CORRECT answer is:
A. II, IV, III, I, V
B. IV, III, V, I, II
C. I, III, II, IV, V
D. I, IV, II, III, V

5. I. In general, staff-line friction reduces the distinctive contribution of staff personnel.
II. The conflicts, however, introduce an uncontrolled element into the managerial system.
III. On the other hand, the natural resistance of the line to staff innovations probably usefully restrains over-eager efforts to apply untested procedures on a large scale.
IV. Under such conditions, it is difficult to know when valuable ideas are being sacrificed.
V. The relatively weak position of staff, requiring accommodation to the line, tends to restrict their ability to engage in free, experimental innovation.

The CORRECT answer is:
A. IV, II, III, I, V
B. I, V, III, II, IV
C. V, III, I, II, IV
D. II, I, IV, V, III

KEY (CORRECT ANSWERS)

1. A
2. D
3. D
4. A
5. B

TEST 3

DIRECTIONS: Questions 1 through 4 consist of six sentences which can be arranged in a logical sequence. For each question, select the choice which places the numbered sentences in the MOST logical sequent. *PRINT THE LETTER OF THE CORRECT ANSWER IN THE SPACE AT THE RIGHT.*

1. I. The burden of proof as to each issue is determined before trial and remains upon the same party throughout the trial.
    II. The jury is at liberty to believe one witness' testimony as against a number of contradictory witnesses.
    III. In a civil case, the party bearing the burden of proof is required to prove his contention by a fair preponderance of the evidence.
    IV. However, it must be noted that a fair preponderance of evidence does not necessarily mean a greater number of witnesses.
    V. The burden of proof is the burden which rests upon one of the parties to an action to persuade the trier of the facts, generally the jury, that a proposition he asserts is true.
    VI. If the evidence is equally balanced, or if it leaves the jury in such doubt as to be unable to decide the controversy either way, judgment must be given against the party upon whom the burden of proof rests.
    The CORRECT answer is:
    A. III, II, V, IV, I, VI
    B. I, II, VI, V, III, IV
    C. III, IV, V, I, II, VI
    D. V, I, III, VI, IV, II

    1.____

2. I. If a parent is without assets and is unemployed, he cannot be convicted of the crime of non-support of a child.
    II. The term "sufficient ability" has been held to mean sufficient financial ability.
    III. It does not matter if his unemployment is by choice or unavoidable circumstances.
    IV. If he fails to take any steps at all, he may be liable to prosecution for endangering the welfare of a child.
    V. Under the penal law, a parent is responsible for the support of his minor child only if the parent is "of sufficient ability."
    VI. An indigent parent may meet his obligation by borrowing money or by seeking aid under the provisions of the Social Welfare Law.
    The CORRECT answer is:
    A. VI, I, V, III, II, IV
    B. I, III, V, II, IV, VI
    C. V, II, I, III, VI, IV
    D. I, VI, IV, V, II, III

    2.____

3. I. Consider, for example, the case of a rabble rouser who urges a group of twenty people to go out and break the windows of a nearby factory.
    II. Therefore, the law fills the indicated gap with the crime of inciting to riot.
    III. A person is considered guilty of inciting to riot when he urges ten or more persons to engage in tumultuous and violent conduct of a kind likely to create public alarm.
    IV. However, if he has not obtained the cooperation of at least four people, he cannot be charged with unlawful assembly.

    3.____

149

2 (#3)

V. The charge of inciting to riot was added to the law to cover types of conduct which cannot be classified as either the crime of "riot" or the crime of "unlawful assembly."
VI. If he acquires the acquiescence of at least four of them, he is guilty of unlawful assembly even if the project does not materialize.

The CORRECT answer is:
A. III, V, I, VI, IV, II
B. V, I, IV, VI, II, III
C. III, IV, I, V, II, VI
D. V, I, IV, VI, III, II

4. I. If, however, the rebuttal evidence presents an issue of credibility, it is for the jury to determine whether the presumption has, in fact, been destroyed.
II. Once sufficient evidence to the contrary is introduced, the presumption disappears from the trial.
III. The effect of a presumption is to place the burden upon the adversary to come forward with evidence to rebut the presumption.
IV. When a presumption is overcome and ceases to exist in the case, the fact or facts which gave rise to the presumption still remain.
V. Whether a presumption has been overcome is ordinarily a question for the court.
VI. Such information may furnish a basis for a logical inference.

The CORRECT answer is:
A. IV, VI, II, V, I, III
B. III, II, V, I, IV, VI
C. V, III, VI, IV, II, I
D. V, IV, I, II, VI, III

4.____

KEY (CORRECT ANSWERS)

1. D
2. C
3. A
4. B

RECORD KEEPING
EXAMINATION SECTION
TEST 1

DIRECTIONS: Each question or incomplete statement is followed by several suggested answers or completions. Select the one that BEST answers the question or completes the statement. *PRINT THE LETTER OF THE CORRECT ANSWER IN THE SPACE AT THE RIGHT.*

Questions 1-7.

DIRECTIONS: In answering Questions 1 through 7, use the following master list. For each question, determine where the name would fit on the master list. Each answer choice indicates right before or after the name in the answer choice.

    Aaron, Jane
    Armstead, Brendan
    Bailey, Charles
    Dent, Ricardo
    Grant, Mark
    Mars, Justin
    Methieu, Justine
    Parker, Cathy
    Sampson, Suzy
    Thomas, Heather

1. Schmidt, William
   A. Right before Cathy Parker
   B. Right after Heather Thomas
   C. Right after Suzy Sampson
   D. Right before Ricardo Dent

1.____

2. Asanti, Kendall
   A. Right before Jane Aaron
   B. Right after Charles Bailey
   C. Right before Justine Methieu
   D. Right after Brendan Armstead

2.____

3. O'Brien, Daniel
   A. Right after Justine Methieu
   B. Right before Jane Aaron
   C. Right after Mark Grant
   D. Right before Suzy Sampson

3.____

4. Marrow, Alison
   A. Right before Cathy Parker
   B. Right before Justin Mars
   C. Right before Mark Grant
   D. Right after Heather Thomas

4.____

5. Grantt, Marissa
   A. Right before Mark Grant
   B. Right after Mark Grant
   C. Right after Justin Mars
   D. Right before Suzy Sampson

5.____

6. Thompson, Heath 6.____
   A. Right after Justin Mars
   B. Right before Suzy Sampson
   C. Right after Heather Thomas
   D. Right before Cathy Parker

DIRECTIONS: Before answering Question 7, add in all of the names from Questions 1 through 6. Then fit the name in alphabetical order based on the new list.

7. Francisco, Mildred 7.____
   A. Right before Mark Grant
   B. Right after Marissa Grantt
   C. Right before Alison Marrow
   D. Right after Kendall Asanti

Questions 8-10.

DIRECTIONS: In answering Questions 8 through 10, compare each pair of names and addresses. Indicate whether they are the same or different in any way.

8. William H. Pratt, J.D.   William H. Pratt, J.D. 8.____
   Attourney at Law   Attorney at Law
   A. No differences
   B. 1 difference
   C. 2 differences
   D. 3 differences

9. 1303 Theater Drive,; Apt. 3-B   1330 Theatre Drive,; Apt. 3-B 9.____
   A. No differences
   B. 1 difference
   C. 2 differences
   D. 3 differences

10. Petersdorff, Briana and Mary   Petersdorff, Briana and Mary 10.____
    A. No differences
    B. 1 difference
    C. 2 differences
    D. 3 differences

11. Which of the following words, if any, are misspelled? 11.____
    A. Affordable
    B. Circumstansial
    C. Legalese
    D. None of the above

Questions 12-13.

DIRECTIONS: Questions 12 and 13 are to be answered on the basis of the following table.

Standardized Test Results for High School Students in District #1230

	English	Math	Science	Reading
High School 1	21	22	15	18
High School 2	12	16	13	15
High School 3	16	18	21	17
High School 4	19	14	15	16

The scores for each high school in the district were averaged out and listed for each subject tested. Scores of 0-10 are significantly below College Readiness Standards. 11-15 are below College Readiness, 16-20 meet College Readiness, and 21-25 are above College Readiness.

12. If the high schools need to meet or exceed in at least half the categories in order to NOT be considered "at risk," which schools are considered "at risk"? 12.____
    A. High School 2
    B. High School 3
    C. High School 4
    D. Both A and C

13. What percentage of subjects did the district as a whole meet or exceed College Readiness standards? 13.____
    A. 25%   B. 50%   C. 75%   D. 100%

Questions 14-15.

DIRECTIONS: Questions 14 and 15 are to be answered on the basis of the following information.

You have seven employees working as a part of your team: Austin, Emily, Jeremy, Christina, Martin, Harriet, and Steve. You have just sent an e-mail informing them that there will be a mandatory training session next week. To ensure that work still gets done, you are offering the training twice during the week: once on Tuesday and also on Thursday. This way half the employees will still be working while the other half attend the training. The only other issue is that Jeremy doesn't work on Tuesdays and Harriet doesn't work on Thursdays due to compressed work schedules.

14. Which of the following is a possible attendance roster for the first training session? 14.____
    A. Emily, Jeremy, Steve
    B. Steve, Christina, Harriet
    C. Harriet, Jeremy, Austin
    D. Steve, Martin, Jeremy

15. If Harriet, Christina, and Steve attend the training session on Tuesday, which of the following is a possible roster for Thursday's training session? 15.____
    A. Jeremy, Emily, and Austin
    B. Emily, Martin, and Harriet
    C. Austin, Christina, and Emily
    D. Jeremy, Emily, and Steve

Questions 16-20.

DIRECTIONS: In answering Questions 16 through 20, you will be given a word and will need to choose the answer choice that is MOST similar or different to the word.

16. Which word means the SAME as *annual*? 16.____
    A. Monthly   B. Usually   C. Yearly   D. Constantly

17. Which word means the SAME as *effort*? 17.____
    A. Energy   B. Equate   C. Cherish   D. Commence

18. Which word means the OPPOSITE of *forlorn*? 18.____
    A. Neglected   B. Lethargy   C. Optimistic   D. Astonished

19. Which word means the SAME as *risk*? 19.____
    A. Admire   B. Hazard   C. Limit   D. Hesitant

20. Which word means the OPPOSITE of *translucent*? 20._____
    A. Opaque B. Transparent C. Luminous D. Introverted

21. Last year, Jamie's annual salary was $50,000. Her boss called her today 21._____
    to inform her that she would receive a 20% raise for the upcoming year. How
    much more money will Jamie receive next year?
    A. $60,000 B. $10,000 C. $1,000 D. $51,000

22. You and a co-worker work for a temp hiring agency as part of their office 22._____
    staff. You both are given 6 days off per month. How many days off are you
    and your co-worker given in a year?
    A. 24 B. 72 C. 144 D. 48

23. If Margot makes $34,000 per year and she works 40 hours per week for 23._____
    all 52 weeks, what is her hourly rate?
    A. $16.34/hour B. $17.00/hour C. $15.54/hour D. $13.23/hour

24. How many dimes are there in $175.00? 24._____
    A. 175 B. 1,750 C. 3,500 D. 17,500

25. If Janey is three times as old as Emily, and Emily is 3, how old is Janey? 25._____
    A. 6 B. 9 C. 12 D. 15

KEY (CORRECT ANSWERS)

1.	C	11.	B
2.	D	12.	A
3.	A	13.	D
4.	B	14.	B
5.	B	15.	A
6.	C	16.	C
7.	A	17.	A
8.	B	18.	C
9.	C	19.	B
10.	A	20.	A

21. B
22. C
23. A
24. B
25. B

TEST 2

DIRECTIONS: Each question or incomplete statement is followed by several suggested answers or completions. Select the one that BEST answers the question or completes the statement. *PRINT THE LETTER OF THE CORRECT ANSWER IN THE SPACE AT THE RIGHT.*

Questions 1-6.

DIRECTIONS: Questions 1 through 6 are to be answered on the basis of the following information.

item	name of item to be ordered
quantity	minimum number that can be ordered
beginning amount	amount in stock at start of month
amount received	amount receiving during month
ending amount	amount in stock at end of month
amount used	amount used during month
amount to order	will need at least as much of each item as used in the previous month
unit price	cost of each unit of an item
total price	total price for the order

Item	Quantity	Beginning	Received	Ending	Amount Used	Amount to Order	Unit Price	Total Price
Pens	10	22	10	8	24	20	$0.11	$2.20
Spiral notebooks	8	30	13	12			$0.25	
Binder clips	2 boxes	3 boxes	1 box	1 box			$1.79	
Sticky notes	3 packs	12 packs	4 packs	2 packs			$1.29	
Dry erase markers	1 pack (dozen)	34 markers	8 markers	40 markers			$16.49	
Ink cartridges (printer)	1 cartridge	3 cartridges	1 cartridge	2 cartridges			$79.99	
Folders	10 folders	25 folders	15 folders	10 folders			$1.08	

1. How many packs of sticky notes were used during the month? 1.____
   A. 16   B. 10   C. 12   D. 14

2. How many folders need to be ordered for next month? 2.____
   A. 15   B. 20   C. 30   D. 40

3. What is the total price of notebooks that you will need to order? 3.____
   A. $6.00   B. $0.25   C. $4.50   D. $2.75

4. Which of the following will you spend the second most money on? 4.____
   A. Ink cartridges   B. Dry erase markers
   C. Sticky notes   D. Binder clips

5. How many packs of dry erase markers should you order? 5.____
   A. 1   B. 8   C. 12   D. 0

6. What will be the total price of the file folders you order? 6.____
   A. $20.16   B. $21.60   C. $10.80   D. $4.32

Questions 7-11.

DIRECTIONS: Questions 7 through 11 are to be answered on the basis of the following table.

| Number of Car Accidents, By Location and Cause, for 2014 | | | | | | |
| Cause | Location 1 | | Location 2 | | Location 3 | |
	Number	Percent	Number	Percent	Number	Percent
Severe Weather	10		25		30	
Excessive Speeding	20	40	5		10	
Impaired Driving	15		15	25	8	
Miscellaneous	5		15		2	4
TOTALS	50	100	60	100	50	100

7. Which of the following is the third highest cause of accidents for all three locations? 7.____
   A. Severe Weather
   B. Impaired Driving
   C. Miscellaneous
   D. Excessive Speeding

8. The average number of Severe Weather accidents per week at Location 3 for the year (52 weeks) was MOST NEARLY 8.____
   A. 0.57   B. 30   C. 1   D. 1.25

9. Which location had the LARGEST percentage of accidents caused by Impaired Driving? 9.____
   A. 1   B. 2   C. 3   D. Both A and B

10. If one-third of the accidents at all three locations resulted in at least one fatality, what is the LEAST amount of deaths caused by accidents last year? 10.____
    A. 60   B. 106   C. 66   D. 53

11. What is the percentage of accidents caused by miscellaneous means from all three locations in 2014? 11.____
    A. 5%   B. 10%   C. 13%   D. 25%

12. How many pairs of the following groups of letters are exactly alike? 12.____
    ACDOBJ   ACDBOJ
    HEWBWR   HEWRWB
    DEERVS   DEERVS
    BRFQSX   BRFQSX
    WEYRVB   WEYRVB
    SPQRZA   SQRPZA

    A. 2   B. 3   C. 4   D. 5

3 (#2)

Questions 13-19.

DIRECTIONS: Questions 13 through 19 are to be answered on the basis of the following information.

In 2012, the most current information on the American population was finished. The information was compiled by 200 volunteers in each of the 50 states. The territory of Puerto Rico, a sovereign of the United States, had 25 people assigned to compile data. In February of 2010, volunteers in each state and sovereign began collecting information. In Puerto Rico, data collection finished by January 31st, 2011, while work in the United States was completed on June 30, 2012. Each volunteer gathered data on the population of their state or sovereign. When the information was compiled, volunteers sent reports to the nation's capital, Washington, D.C. Each volunteer worked 20 hours per month and put together 10 reports per month. After the data was compiled in total, 50 people reviewed the data and worked from January 2012 to December 2012.

13. How many reports were generated from February 2010 to April 2010 in Illinois and Ohio?
    A. 3,000   B. 6,000   C. 12,000   D. 15,000

14. How many volunteers in total collected population data in January 2012?
    A. 10,000   B. 2,000   C. 225   D. 200

15. How many reports were put together in May 2012?
    A. 2,000   B. 50,000   C. 100,000   D. 100,250

16. How many hours did the Puerto Rican volunteers work in the fall (September-November)?
    A. 60   B. 500   C. 1,500   D. 0

17. How many workers were compiling or reviewing data in July 2012?
    A. 25   B. 50   C. 200   D. 250

18. What was the total amount of hours worked by Nevada volunteers in July 2010?
    A. 500   B. 4,000   C. 4,500   D. 5,000

19. How many reviewers worked in January 2013?
    A. 75   B. 50   C. 0   D. 25

20. John has to file 10 documents per shelf. How many documents would it take for John to fill 40 shelves?
    A. 40   B. 400   C. 4,500   D. 5,000

21. Jill wants to travel from New York City to Los Angeles by bike, which is approximately 2,772 miles. How many miles per day would Jill need to average if she wanted to complete the trip in 4 weeks?
    A. 100   B. 89   C. 99   D. 94

22. If there are 24 CPU's and only 7 monitors, how many more monitors do you need to have the same amount of monitors as CPU's?
    A. Not enough information
    B. 17
    C. 31
    D. 0

22.____

23. If Gerry works 5 days a week and 8 hours each day, and John works 3 days a week and 10 hours each day, how many more hours per year will Gerry work than John?
    A. They work the same amount of hours.
    B. 450
    C. 520
    D. 832

23.____

24. Jimmy gets transferred to a new office. The new office has 25 employees, but only 16 are there due to a blizzard. How many coworkers was Jimmy able to meet on his first day?
    A. 16   B. 25   C. 9   D. 7

24.____

25. If you do a fundraiser for charities in your area and raise $500 total, how much would you give to each charity if you were donating equal amounts to 3 of them?
    A. $250.00   B. $167.77   C. $50.00   D. $111.11

25.____

KEY (CORRECT ANSWERS)

1.	D		11.	C
2.	B		12.	B
3.	A		13.	C
4.	C		14.	A
5.	D		15.	C
6.	B		16.	C
7.	D		17.	B
8.	A		18.	B
9.	A		19.	C
10.	D		20.	B

21. C
22. B
23. C
24. A
25. B

TEST 3

DIRECTIONS: Each question or incomplete statement is followed by several suggested answers or completions. Select the one that BEST answers the question or completes the statement. *PRINT THE LETTER OF THE CORRECT ANSWER IN THE SPACE AT THE RIGHT.*

Questions 1-3.

DIRECTIONS: In answering Questions 1 through 3, choose the correctly spelled word.

1. A. allusion B. alusion C. allusien D. allution 1.____

2. A. altitude B. alltitude C. atlitude D. altlitude 2.____

3. A. althogh B. allthough C. althrough D. although 3.____

Questions 4-9.

DIRECTIONS: In answering Questions 4 through 9, choose the answer that BEST completes the analogy.

4. Odometer is to mileage as compass is to 4.____
 A. speed B. needle C. hiking D. direction

5. Marathon is to race as hibernation is to 5.____
 A. winter B. dream C. sleep D. bear

6. Cup is to coffee as bowl is to 6.____
 A. dish B. spoon C. food D. soup

7. Flow is to river as stagnant is to 7.____
 A. pool B. rain C. stream D. canal

8. Paw is to cat as hoof is to 8.____
 A. lamb B. horse C. lion D. elephant

9. Architect is to building as sculptor is to 9.____
 A. museum B. chisel C. stone D. statue

159

Questions 10-14.

DIRECTIONS: Questions 10 through 14 are to be answered on the basis of the following graph.

Population of Carroll City Broken Down by Age and Gender (in Thousands)			
Age	Female	Male	Total
Under 15	60	60	120
15-23		22	
24-33		20	44
34-43	13	18	31
44-53	20		67
64 and Over	65	65	130
TOTAL	230	232	462

10. How many people in the city are between the ages of 15-23?   10.____
    A. 70   B. 46,000   C. 70,000   D. 225,000

11. Approximately what percentage of the total population of the city was   11.____
    female aged 24-33?
    A. 10%   B. 5%   C. 15%   D. 25%

12. If 33% of the males have a job and 55% of females don't have a job,   12.____
    which of the following statements is TRUE?
    A. Males have approximately 2,600 more jobs than females.
    B. Females have approximately 49,000 more jobs than males.
    C. Females have approximately 26,000 more jobs than males.
    D. None of the above statements are true.

13. How many females between the ages of 15-23 live in Carroll City?   13.____
    A. 67,000   B. 24,000   C. 48,000   D. 91,000

14. Assume all males 44-53 living in Carroll City are employed. If two-thirds   14.____
    of males age 44-53 work jobs outside of Carroll City, how many work within city
    limits?
    A. 31,333
    B. 15,667
    C. 47,000
    D. Cannot answer the question with the information provided

Questions 15-16.

DIRECTIONS: Questions 15 and 16 are labeled as shown. Alphabetize them for filing. Choose the answer that correctly shows the order.

15. (1) AED
    (2) OOS
    (3) FOA
    (4) DOM
    (5) COB

    A. 2-5-4-3-2   B. 1-4-5-2-3   C. 1-5-4-2-3   D. 1-5-4-3-2

15._____

16. Alphabetize the names of the people. Last names are given last.
    (1) Lindsey Jamestown
    (2) Jane Alberta
    (3) Ally Jamestown
    (4) Allison Johnston
    (5) Lyle Moreno

    A. 2-1-3-4-5   B. 3-4-2-1-5   C. 2-3-1-4-5   D. 4-3-2-1-5

16._____

17. Which of the following words is misspelled?
    A. disgust   B. whisper
    C. locale   D. none of the above

17._____

Questions 18-21.

DIRECTIONS: Questions 18 through 21 are to be answered on the basis of the following list of employees.

Robertson, Aaron
Bacon, Gina
Jerimiah, Trace
Gillette, Stanley
Jacks, Sharon

18. Which employee name would come in third in alphabetized list?
    A. Robertson, Aaron   B. Jerimiah, Trace
    C. Gillette, Stanley   D. Jacks, Sharon

18._____

19. Which employee's first name starts with the letter in the alphabet that is five letters after the first letter of their last name?
    A. Jerimiah, Trace   B. Bacon, Gina
    C. Jacks, Sharon   D. Gillette, Stanley

19._____

20. How many employees have last names that are exactly five letters long?
    A. 1   B. 2   C. 3   D. 4

20._____

21. How many of the employees have either a first or last name that starts with the letter "G"? 21.____
    A. 1   B. 2   C. 4   D. 5

Questions 22-25.

DIRECTIONS: Questions 22 through 25 are to be answered on the basis of the following chart.

Bicycle Sales (Model #34JA32)							
Country	May	June	July	August	September	October	Total
Germany	34	47	45	54	56	60	296
Britain	40	44	36	47	47	46	260
Ireland	37	32	32	32	34	33	200
Portugal	14	14	14	16	17	14	89
Italy	29	29	28	31	29	31	177
Belgium	22	24	24	26	25	23	144
Total	176	198	179	206	208	207	1166

22. What percentage of the overall total was sold to the German importer? 22.____
    A. 25.3%   B. 22%   C. 24.1%   D. 23%

23. What percentage of the overall total was sold in September? 23.____
    A. 24.1%   B. 25.6%   C. 17.9%   D. 24.6%

24. What is the average number of units per month imported into Belgium over the first four months shown? 24.____
    A. 26   B. 20   C. 24   D. 31

25. If you look at the three smallest importers, what is their total import percentage? 25.____
    A. 35.1%   B. 37.1%   C. 40%   D. 28%

KEY (CORRECT ANSWERS)

1.	A	11.	B
2.	A	12.	C
3.	D	13.	C
4.	D	14.	B
5.	C	15.	D
6.	D	16.	C
7.	A	17.	D
8.	B	18.	D
9.	D	19.	B
10.	C	20.	B

21.	B
22.	A
23.	C
24.	C
25.	A

TEST 4

DIRECTIONS: Each question or incomplete statement is followed by several suggested answers or completions. Select the one that BEST answers the question or completes the statement. *PRINT THE LETTER OF THE CORRECT ANSWER IN THE SPACE AT THE RIGHT.*

Questions 1-6.

DIRECTIONS: In answering Questions 1 through 6, choose the sentence that represents the BEST example of English grammar.

1. A. Joey and me want to go on a vacation next week. 1.____
   B. Gary told Jim he would need to take some time off.
   C. If turning six years old, Jim's uncle would teach Spanish to him.
   D. Fax a copy of your resume to Ms. Perez and me.

2. A. Jerry stood in line for almost two hours. 2.____
   B. The reaction to my engagement was less exciting than I thought it would be.
   C. Carlos and me have done great work on this project.
   D. Two parts of the speech needs to be revised before tomorrow.

3. A. Arriving home, the alarm was tripped. 3.____
   B. Jonny is regarded as a stand up guy, a responsible parent, and he doesn't give up until a task is finished.
   C. Each employee must submit a drug test each month.
   D. One of the documents was incinerated in the explosion.

4. A. As soon as my parents get home, I told them I finished all of my chores. 4.____
   B. I asked my teacher to send me my missing work, check my absences, and how did I do on my test.
   C. Matt attempted to keep it concealed from Jenny and me.
   D. If Mary or him cannot get work done on time, I will have to split them up.

5. A. Driving to work, the traffic report warned him of an accident on Highway 47. 5.____
   B. Jimmy has performed well this season.
   C. Since finishing her degree, several job offers have been given to Cam.
   D. Our boss is creating unstable conditions for we employees.

6. A. The thief was described as a tall man with a wiry mustache weighing approximately 150 pounds. 6.____
   B. She gave Patrick and I some more time to finish our work.
   C. One of the books that he ordered was damaged in shipping.
   D. While talking on the rotary phone, the car Jim was driving skidded off the road.

164

Questions 7-9.

DIRECTIONS: Questions 7 through 9 are to be answered on the basis of the following graph.

Ice Lake Frozen Flight (2002-2013)		
Year	Number of Participants	Temperature (Fahrenheit)
2002	22	4°
2003	50	33°
2004	69	18°
2005	104	22°
2006	108	24°
2007	288	33°
2008	173	9°
2009	598	39°
2010	698	26°
2011	696	30°
2012	777	28°
2013	578	32°

7. Which two year span had the LARGEST difference between temperatures? 7.____
   A. 2002 and 2003
   B. 2011 and 2012
   C. 2008 and 2009
   D. 2003 and 2004

8. How many total people participated in the years after the temperature reached at least 29°? 8.____
   A. 2,295
   B. 1,717
   C. 2,210
   D. 4,543

9. In 2007, the event saw 288 participants, while in 2008 that number dropped to 173. Which of the following reasons BEST explains the drop in participants? 9.____
   A. The event had not been going on that long and people didn't know about it.
   B. The lake water wasn't cold enough to have people jump in.
   C. The temperature was too cold for many people who would have normally participated.
   D. None of the above reasons explain the drop in participants.

10. In the following list of numbers, how many times does 4 come just after 2 when 2 comes just after an odd number? 10.____
    2365247653898632488572486392424
    A. 2
    B. 3
    C. 4
    D. 5

11. Which choice below lists the letter that is as far after B as S is after N in the alphabet? 11.____
    A. G
    B. H
    C. I
    D. J

Questions 12-15.

DIRECTIONS: Questions 12 through 15 are to be answered on the basis of the following directory and list of changes.

Directory		
Name	Emp. Type	Position
Julie Taylor	Warehouse	Packer
James King	Office	Administrative Assistant
John Williams	Office	Salesperson
Ray Moore	Warehouse	Maintenance
Kathleen Byrne	Warehouse	Supervisor
Amy Jones	Office	Salesperson
Paul Jonas	Office	Salesperson
Lisa Wong	Warehouse	Loader
Eugene Lee	Office	Accountant
Bruce Lavine	Office	Manager
Adam Gates	Warehouse	Packer
Will Suter	Warehouse	Packer
Gary Lorper	Office	Accountant
Jon Adams	Office	Salesperson
Susannah Harper	Office	Salesperson

Directory Updates:
- Employee e-mail addresses will adhere to the following guidelines: lastnamefirstname@apexindustries.com (ex. Susannah Harper is harpersusannah@apexindustries.com). Currently, employees in the warehouse share one e-mail, distribution@apexindustries.com.
- The "Loader" position will now be referred to as "Specialist I"
- Adam Gates has accepted a Supervisor position within the Warehouse and is no longer a Packer. All warehouse employees report to the two Supervisors and all office employees report to the Manager.

12. Amy Jones tried to send an e-mail to Adam Gates, but it wouldn't send. Which of the following offers the BEST explanation?
    A. Amy put Adam's first name first and then his last name.
    B. Adam doesn't check his e-mail, so he wouldn't know if he received the e-mail or not.
    C. Adam does not have his own e-mail.
    D. Office employees are not allowed to send e-mails to each other.

12.____

13. How many Packers currently work for Apex Industries?
    A. 2   B. 3   C. 4   D. 5

13.____

14. What position does Lisa Wong currently hold?
    A. Specialist I   B. Secretary
    C. Administrative Assistant   D. Loader

14.____

15. If an employee wanted to contact the office manager, which of the following e-mails should the e-mail be sent to? 15._____
    A. officemanager@apexindustries.com
    B. brucelavine@apexindustries.com
    C. lavinebruce@apexindustries.com
    D. distribution@apexindustries.com

Questions 16-19.

DIRECTIONS: In answering Questions 16 through 19, compare the three names, numbers or addresses.

16. Smiley Yarnell   Smiley Yarnel   Smily Yarnell   16._____
    A. All three are exactly alike.
    B. The first and second are exactly alike.
    C. The second and third are exactly alike.
    D. All three are different.

17. 1583 Theater Drive   1583 Theater Drive   1583 Theatre Drive   17._____
    A. All three are exactly alike.
    B. The first and second are exactly alike.
    C. The second and third are exactly alike.
    D. All three are different.

18. 3341893212   3341893212   3341893212   18._____
    A. All three are exactly alike.
    B. The first and second are exactly alike.
    C. The second and third are exactly alike.
    D. All three are different.

19. Douglass Watkins   Douglas Watkins   Douglass Watkins   19._____
    A. All three are exactly alike.
    B. The first and third are exactly alike.
    C. The second and third are exactly alike.
    D. All three are different.

Questions 20-24.

DIRECTIONS: In answering Questions 20 through 24, you will be presented with a word. Choose the synonym that BEST represents the word in question.

20. Flexible   20._____
    A. delicate   B. inflammable   C. strong   D. pliable

21. Alternative   21._____
    A. choice   B. moderate   C. lazy   D. value

5 (#4)

22. Corroborate
    A. examine   B. explain   C. verify   D. explain   22._____

23. Respiration
    A. recovery   B. breathing   C. sweating   D. selfish   23._____

24. Negligent
    A. lazy   B. moderate   C. hopeless   D. lax   24._____

25. Plumber is to Wrench as Painter is to   25._____
    A. pipe   B. shop   C. hammer   D. brush

KEY (CORRECT ANSWERS)

1.	D	11.	A
2.	A	12.	C
3.	D	13.	A
4.	C	14.	A
5.	B	15.	C
6.	C	16.	D
7.	C	17.	B
8.	B	18.	A
9.	C	19.	B
10.	C	20.	D

21. A
22. C
23. B
24. D
25. D

PHILOSOPHY, PRINCIPLES, PRACTICES, AND TECHNICS OF SUPERVISION, ADMINISTRATION, MANAGEMENT, AND ORGANIZATION

TABLE OF CONTENTS

	Page
MEANING OF SUPERVISION	1
THE OLD AND THE NEW SUPERVISION	1
THE EIGHT (8) BASIC PRINCIPLES OF THE NEW SUPERVISION	1
I. Principle of Responsibility	1
II. Principle of Authority	2
III. Principle of Self-Growth	2
IV. Principle of Individual Worth	2
V. Principle of Creative Leadership	2
VI. Principle of Success and Failure	2
VII. Principle of Science	3
VIII. Principle of Cooperation	3
WHAT IS ADMINISTRATION?	3
I. Practices Commonly Classed as "Supervisory"	3
II. Practices Commonly Classed as "Administrative"	3
III. Practices Commonly Classed as Both "Supervisory" and "Administrative"	4
RESPONSIBILITIES OF THE SUPERVISOR	4
COMPETENCIES OF THE SUPERVISOR	4
THE PROFESSIONAL SUPERVISOR-EMPLOYEE RELATIONSHIP	4
MINI-TEXT IN SUPERVISION, ADMINISTRATION, MANAGEMENT, AND ORGANIZATION	5
I. Brief Highlights	5
A. Levels of Management	6
B. What the Supervisor Must Learn	6
C. A Definition of Supervision	6
D. Elements of the Team Concept	6
E. Principles of Organization	6
F. The Four Important Parts of Every Job	7
G. Principles of Delegation	7
H. Principles of Effective Communications	7
I. Principles of Work Improvement	7
J. Areas of Job Improvement	7
K. Seven Key Points in Making Improvements	8

	L.	Corrective Techniques for Job Improvement	8
	M.	A Planning Checklist	8
	N.	Five Characteristics of Good Directions	9
	O.	Types of Directions	9
	P.	Controls	9
	Q.	Orienting the New Employee	9
	R.	Checklist for Orienting New Employees	9
	S.	Principles of Learning	10
	T.	Causes of Poor Performance	10
	U.	Four Major Steps in On-the-Job Instructions	10
	V.	Employees Want Five Things	10
	W.	Some Don'ts in Regard to Praise	11
	X.	How to Gain Your Workers' Confidence	11
	Y.	Sources of Employee Problems	11
	Z.	The Supervisor's Key to Discipline	11
	AA.	Five Important Processes of Management	12
	BB.	When the Supervisor Fails to Plan	12
	CC.	Fourteen General Principles of Management	12
	DD.	Change	12
II.	Brief Topical Summaries		13
	A.	Who/What is the Supervisor?	13
	B.	The Sociology of Work	13
	C.	Principles and Practices of Supervision	14
	D.	Dynamic Leadership	14
	E.	Processes for Solving Problems	15
	F.	Training for Results	15
	G.	Health, Safety, and Accident Prevention	16
	H.	Equal Employment Opportunity	16
	I.	Improving Communications	16
	J.	Self-Development	17
	K.	Teaching and Training	17
		1. The Teaching Process	17
		a. Preparation	17
		b. Presentation	18
		c. Summary	18
		d. Application	18
		e. Evaluation	18
		2. Teaching Methods	18
		a. Lecture	18
		b. Discussion	18
		c. Demonstration	19
		d. Performance	19
		e. Which Method to Use	19

PHILOSOPHY, PRINCIPLES, PRACTICES, AND TECHNICS
OF
SUPERVISION, ADMINISTRATION, MANAGEMENT, AND ORGANIZATION

MEANING OF SUPERVISION

The extension of the democratic philosophy has been accompanied by an extension in the scope of supervision. Modern leaders and supervisors no longer think of supervision in the narrow sense of being confined chiefly to visiting employees, supplying materials, or rating the staff. They regard supervision as being intimately related to all the concerned agencies of society, they speak of the supervisor's function in terms of "growth," rather than the "improvement" of employees.

This modern concept of supervision may be defined as follows: Supervision is leadership and the development of leadership within groups which are cooperatively engaged in inspection, research, training, guidance, and evaluation.

THE OLD AND THE NEW SUPERVISION

TRADITIONAL
1. Inspection
2. Focused on the employee
3. Visitation
4. Random and haphazard
5. Imposed and authoritarian
6. One person usually

MODERN
1. Study and analysis
2. Focused on aims, materials, methods, supervisors, employees, environment
3. Demonstrations, intervisitation, workshops, directed reading, bulletins, etc.
4. Definitely organized and planned (scientific)
5. Cooperative and democratic
6. Many persons involved (creative)

THE EIGHT (8) BASIC PRINCIPLES OF THE NEW SUPERVISION

I. Principle of Responsibility
   Authority to act and responsibility for acting must be joined.
   A. If you give responsibility, give authority.
   B. Define employee duties clearly.
   C. Protect employees from criticism by others.
   D. Recognize the rights as well as obligations of employees.
   E. Achieve the aims of a democratic society insofar as it is possible within the area of your work.
   F. Establish a situation favorable to training and learning.
   G. Accept ultimate responsibility for everything done in your section, unit, office, division, department.
   H. Good administration and good supervision are inseparable.

II. Principle of Authority
The success of the supervisor is measured by the extent to which the power of authority is not used.
   A. Exercise simplicity and informality in supervision
   B. Use the simplest machinery of supervision
   C. If it is good for the organization as a whole, it is probably justified.
   D. Seldom be arbitrary or authoritative.
   E. Do not base your work on the power of position or of personality.
   F. Permit and encourage the free expression of opinions.

III. Principle of Self-Growth
The success of the supervisor is measured by the extent to which, and the speed with which, he is no longer needed.
   A. Base criticism on principles, not on specifics.
   B. Point out higher activities to employees.
   C. Train for self-thinking by employees to meet new situations.
   D. Stimulate initiative, self-reliance, and individual responsibility
   E. Concentrate on stimulating the growth of employees rather than on removing defects.

IV. Principle of Individual Worth
Respect for the individual is a paramount consideration in supervision.
   A. Be human and sympathetic in dealing with employees.
   B. Don't nag about things to be done.
   C. Recognize the individual differences among employees and seek opportunities to permit best expression of each personality.

V. Principle of Creative Leadership
The best supervision is that which is not apparent to the employee.
   A. Stimulate, don't drive employees to creative action.
   B. Emphasize doing good things.
   C. Encourage employees to do what they do best.
   D. Do not be too greatly concerned with details of subject or method.
   E. Do not be concerned exclusively with immediate problems and activities.
   F. Reveal higher activities and make them both desired and maximally possible.
   G. Determine procedures in the light of each situation but see that these are derived from a sound basic philosophy.
   H. Aid, inspire, and lead so as to liberate the creative spirit latent in all good employees.

VI. Principle of Success and Failure
There are no unsuccessful employees, only unsuccessful supervisors who have failed to give proper leadership.
   A. Adapt suggestions to the capacities, attitudes, and prejudices of employees.
   B. Be gradual, be progressive, be persistent.
   C. Help the employee find the general principle; have the employee apply his own problem to the general principle.
   D. Give adequate appreciation for good work and honest effort.
   E. Anticipate employee difficulties and help to prevent them.
   F. Encourage employees to do the desirable things they will do anyway.
   G. Judge your supervision by the results it secures.

VII. Principle of Science
Successful supervision is scientific, objective, and experimental. It is based on facts, not on prejudices.
   A. Be cumulative in results.
   B. Never divorce your suggestions from the goals of training.
   C. Don't be impatient of results.
   D. Keep all matters on a professional, not a personal, level.
   E. Do not be concerned exclusively with immediate problems and activities.
   F. Use objective means of determining achievement and rating where possible.

VIII. Principle of Cooperation
Supervision is a cooperative enterprise between supervisor and employee.
   A. Begin with conditions as they are.
   B. Ask opinions of all involved when formulating policies.
   C. Organization is as good as its weakest link.
   D. Let employees help to determine policies and department programs.
   E. Be approachable and accessible—physically and mentally.
   F. Develop pleasant social relationships.

WHAT IS ADMINISTRATION

Administration is concerned with providing the environment, the material facilities, and the operational procedures that will promote the maximum growth and development of supervisors and employees. (Organization is an aspect and a concomitant of administration.)

There is no sharp line of demarcation between supervision and administration; these functions are intimately interrelated and, often, overlapping. They are complementary activities.

I. Practices Commonly Classed as "Supervisory"
   A. Conducting employees' conferences
   B. Visiting sections, units, offices, divisions, departments
   C. Arranging for demonstrations
   D. Examining plans
   E. Suggesting professional reading
   F. Interpreting bulletins
   G. Recommending in-service training courses
   H. Encouraging experimentation
   I. Appraising employee morale
   J. Providing for intervisitation

II. Practices Commonly Classified as "Administrative"
   A. Management of the office
   B. Arrangement of schedules for extra duties
   C. Assignment of rooms or areas
   D. Distribution of supplies
   E. Keeping records and reports
   F. Care of audio-visual materials
   G. Keeping inventory records
   H. Checking record cards and books

      I. Programming special activities
      J. Checking on the attendance and punctuality of employees

III. Practices Commonly Classified as Both "Supervisory" and "Administrative"
    A. Program construction
    B. Testing or evaluating outcomes
    C. Personnel accounting
    D. Ordering instructional materials

RESPONSIBILITIES OF THE SUPERVISOR

A person employed in a supervisory capacity must constantly be able to improve his own efficiency and ability. He represent the employer to the employees and only continuous self-examination can make him a capable supervisor.

Leadership and training are the supervisor's responsibility. An efficient working unit is one in which the employees work with the supervisor. It is his job to bring out the best in his employees. He must always be relaxed, courteous, and calm in his association with his employees. Their feelings are important, and a harsh attitude does not develop the most efficient employees.

COMPETENCES OF THE SUPERVISOR

    I. Complete knowledge of the duties and responsibilities of his position.
    II. To be able to organize a job, plan ahead, and carry through.
    III. To have self-confidence and initiative.
    IV. To be able to handle the unexpected situation and make quick decisions.
    V. To be able to properly train subordinates in the positions they are best suited for.
    VI. To be able to keep good human relations among his subordinates.
    VII. To be able to keep good human relations between his subordinates and himself and to earn their respect and trust.

THE PROFESSIONAL SUPERVISOR-EMPLOYEE RELATIONSHIP

There are two kinds of efficiency: one kind is only apparent and is produced in organizations through the exercise of mere discipline; this is but a simulation of the second, or true, efficiency which springs from spontaneous cooperation. If you are a manager, no matter how great or small your responsibility, it is your job, in the final analysis, to create and develop this involuntary cooperation among the people whom you supervise. For, no matter how powerful a combination of money, machines, and materials a company may have, this is a dead and sterile thing without a team of willing, thinking, and articulate people to guide it.

The following 21 points are presented as indicative of the exemplary basic relationship that should exist between supervisor and employee:

1. Each person wants to be liked and respected by his fellow employee and wants to be treated with consideration and respect by his superior.
2. The most competent employee will make an error. However, in a unit where good relations exist between the supervisor and his employees, tenseness and fear do not exist. Thus, errors are not hidden or covered up, and the efficiency of a unit is not impaired.

3. Subordinates resent rules, regulations, or orders that are unreasonable or unexplained.
4. Subordinates are quick to resent unfairness, harshness, injustices, and favoritism.
5. An employee will accept responsibility if he knows that he will be complimented for a job well done, and not too harshly chastised for failure; that his supervisor will check the cause of the failure, and, if it was the supervisor's fault, he will assume the blame therefore. If it was the employee's fault, his supervisor will explain the correct method or means of handling the responsibility.
6. An employee wants to receive credit for a suggestion he has made, that is used. If a suggestion cannot be used, the employee is entitled to an explanation. The supervisor should not say "no" and close the subject.
7. Fear and worry slow up a worker's ability. Poor working environment can impair his physical and mental health. A good supervisor avoids forceful methods, threats, and arguments to get a job done.
8. A forceful supervisor is able to train his employees individually and as a team, and is able to motivate them in the proper channels.
9. A mature supervisor is able to properly evaluate his subordinates and to keep them happy and satisfied.
10. A sensitive supervisor will never patronize his subordinates.
11. A worthy supervisor will respect his employees' confidences.
12. Definite and clear-cut responsibilities should be assigned to each executive.
13. Responsibility should always be coupled with corresponding authority.
14. No change should be made in the scope or responsibilities of a position without a definite understanding to that effect on the part of all persons concerned.
15. No executive or employee, occupying a single position in the organization, should be subject to definite orders from more than one source.
16. Orders should never be given to subordinates over the head of a responsible executive. Rather than do this, the officer in question should be supplanted.
17. Criticisms of subordinates should, whoever possible, be made privately, and in no case should a subordinate be criticized in the presence of executives or employees of equal or lower rank.
18. No dispute or difference between executives or employees as to authority or responsibilities should be considered too trivial for prompt and careful adjudication.
19. Promotions, wage changes, and disciplinary action should always be approved by the executive immediately superior to the one directly responsible.
20. No executive or employee should ever be required, or expected, to be at the same time an assistant to, and critic of, another.
21. Any executive whose work is subject to regular inspection should, wherever practicable, be given the assistance and facilities necessary to enable him to maintain an independent check of the quality of his work.

MINI-TEXT IN SUPERVISION, ADMINISTRATION, MANAGEMENT, AND ORGANIZATION

I. Brief Highlights

Listed concisely and sequentially are major headings and important data in the field for quick recall and review.

A. Levels of Management
Any organization of some size has several levels of management. In terms of a ladder, the levels are:

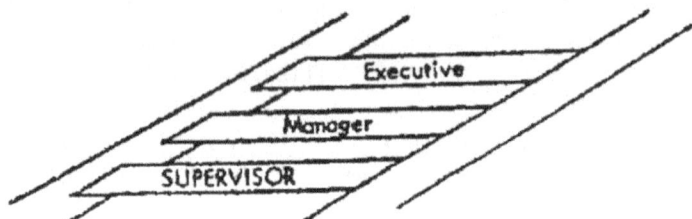

The first level is very important because it is the beginning point of management leadership.

B. What the Supervisor Must Learn
A supervisor must learn to:
1. Deal with people and their differences
2. Get the job done through people
3. Recognize the problems when they exist
4. Overcome obstacles to good performance
5. Evaluate the performance of people
6. Check his own performance in terms of accomplishment

C. A Definition of Supervisor
The term supervisor means any individual having authority, in the interests of the employer, to hire, transfer, suspend, lay-off, recall, promote, discharge, assign, reward, or discipline other employees or responsibility to direct them, or to adjust their grievances, or effectively to recommend such action, if, in connection with the foregoing, exercise of such authority is not of a merely routine or clerical nature but requires the use of independent judgment.

D. Elements of the Team Concept
What is involved in teamwork? The component parts are:
1. Members
2. A leader
3. Goals
4. Plans
5. Cooperation
6. Spirit

E. Principles of Organization
1. A team member must know what his job is.
2. Be sure that the nature and scope of a job are understood.
3. Authority and responsibility should be carefully spelled out.
4. A supervisor should be permitted to make the maximum number of decisions affecting his employees.
5. Employees should report to only one supervisor.
6. A supervisor should direct only as many employees as he can handle effectively.
7. An organization plan should be flexible.

8. Inspection and performance of work should be separate.
9. Organizational problems should receive immediate attention.
10. Assign work in line with ability and experience.

F. The Four Important Parts of Every Job
1. Inherent in every job is the *accountability* for results.
2. A second set of factors in every job is *responsibilities*.
3. Along with duties and responsibilities one must have the *authority* to act within certain limits without obtaining permission to proceed.
4. No job exists in a vacuum. The supervisor is surrounded by key *relationships*.

G. Principles of Delegation
Where work is delegated for the first time, the supervisor should think in terms of these questions:
1. Who is best qualified to do this?
2. Can an employee improve his abilities by doing this?
3. How long should an employee spend on this?
4. Are there any special problems for which he will need guidance?
5. How broad a delegation can I make?

H. Principles of Effective Communications
1. Determine the media.
2. To whom directed?
3. Identification and source authority.
4. Is communication understood?

I. Principles of Work Improvement
1. Most people usually do only the work which is assigned to them.
2. Workers are likely to fit assigned work into the time available to perform it.
3. A good workload usually stimulates output.
4. People usually do their best work when they know that results will be reviewed or inspected.
5. Employees usually feel that someone else is responsible for conditions of work, workplace layout, job methods, type of tools/equipment, and other such factors.
6. Employees are usually defensive about their job security.
7. Employees have natural resistance to change.
8. Employees can support or destroy a supervisor.
9. A supervisor usually earns the respect of his people through his personal example of diligence and efficiency.

J. Areas of Job Improvement
The areas of job improvement are quite numerous, but the most common ones which a supervisor can identify and utilize are:
1. Departmental layout
2. Flow of work
3. Workplace layout
4. Utilization of manpower
5. Work methods
6. Materials handling

7. Utilization
8. Motion economy

K. Seven Key Points in Making Improvements
1. Select the job to be improved
2. Study how it is being done now
3. Question the present method
4. Determine actions to be taken
5. Chart proposed method
6. Get approval and apply
7. Solicit worker participation

L. Corrective Techniques of Job Improvement
Specific Problems
1. Size of workload
2. Inability to meet schedules
3. Strain and fatigue
4. Improper use of men and skills
5. Waste, poor quality, unsafe conditions
6. Bottleneck conditions that hinder output
7. Poor utilization of equipment and machine
8. Efficiency and productivity of labor

General Improvement
1. Departmental layout
2. Flow of work
3. Work plan layout
4. Utilization of manpower
5. Work methods
6. Materials handling
7. Utilization of equipment
8. Motion economy

Corrective Techniques
1. Study with scale model
2. Flow chart study
3. Motion analysis
4. Comparison of units produced to standard allowance
5. Methods analysis
6. Flow chart and equipment study
7. Down time vs. running time
8. Motion analysis

M. A Planning Checklist
1. Objectives
2. Controls
3. Delegations
4. Communications
5. Resources
6. Manpower

7. Equipment
8. Supplies and materials
9. Utilization of time
10. Safety
11. Money
12. Work
13. Timing of improvements

N. Five Characteristics of Good Directions
In order to get results, directions must be:
1. Possible of accomplishment
2. Agreeable with worker interests
3. Related to mission
4. Planned and complete
5. Unmistakably clear

O. Types of Directions
1. Demands or direct orders
2. Requests
3. Suggestion or implication
4. volunteering

P. Controls
A typical listing of the overall areas in which the supervisor should establish controls might be:
1. Manpower
2. Materials
3. Quality of work
4. Quantity of work
5. Time
6. Space
7. Money
8. Methods

Q. Orienting the New Employee
1. Prepare for him
2. Welcome the new employee
3. Orientation for the job
4. Follow-up

R. Checklist for Orienting New Employees   Yes   No
1. Do you appreciate the feelings of new employees
   when they first report for work?   ___   ___
2. Are you aware of the fact that the new employee must
   make a big adjustment to his job?   ___   ___
3. Have you given him good reasons for liking the job and
   the organization?   ___   ___
4. Have you prepared for his first day on the job?   ___   ___
5. Did you welcome him cordially and make him feel needed?   ___   ___

		Yes	No

6. Did you establish rapport with him so that he feels free to talk and discuss matters with you? ___ ___
7. Did you explain his job to him and his relationship to you? ___ ___
8. Does he know that his work will be evaluated periodically on a basis that is fair and objective? ___ ___
9. Did you introduce him to his fellow workers in such a way that they are likely to accept him? ___ ___
10. Does he know what employee benefits he will receive? ___ ___
11. Does he understand the importance of being on the job and what to do if he must leave his duty station? ___ ___
12. Has he been impressed with the importance of accident prevention and safe practice? ___ ___
13. Does he generally know his way around the department? ___ ___
14. Is he under the guidance of a sponsor who will teach the right way of doing things? ___ ___
15. Do you plan to follow-up so that he will continue to adjust successfully to his job? ___ ___

S. Principles of Learning
   1. Motivation
   2. Demonstration or explanation
   3. Practice

T. Causes of Poor Performance
   1. Improper training for job
   2. Wrong tools
   3. Inadequate directions
   4. Lack of supervisory follow-up
   5. Poor communications
   6. Lack of standards of performance
   7. Wrong work habits
   8. Low morale
   9. Other

U. Four Major Steps in On-The-Job Instruction
   1. Prepare the worker
   2. Present the operation
   3. Tryout performance
   4. Follow-up

V. Employees Want Five Things
   1. Security
   2. Opportunity
   3. Recognition
   4. Inclusion
   5. Expression

W. Some Don'ts in Regard to Praise
    1. Don't praise a person for something he hasn't done.
    2. Don't praise a person unless you can be sincere.
    3. Don't be sparing in praise just because your superior withholds it from you.
    4. Don't let too much time elapse between good performance and recognition of it

X. How to Gain Your Workers' Confidence
    Methods of developing confidence include such things as:
    1. Knowing the interests, habits, hobbies of employees
    2. Admitting your own inadequacies
    3. Sharing and telling of confidence in others
    4. Supporting people when they are in trouble
    5. Delegating matters that can be well handled
    6. Being frank and straightforward about problems and working conditions
    7. Encouraging others to bring their problems to you
    8. Taking action on problems which impede worker progress

Y. Sources of Employee Problems
    On-the-job causes might be such things as:
    1. A feeling that favoritism is exercised in assignments
    2. Assignment of overtime
    3. An undue amount of supervision
    4. Changing methods or systems
    5. Stealing of ideas or trade secrets
    6. Lack of interest in job
    7. Threat of reduction in force
    8. Ignorance or lack of communications
    9. Poor equipment
    10. Lack of knowing how supervisor feels toward employee
    11. Shift assignments

    Off-the-job problems might have to do with:
    1. Health
    2. Finances
    3. Housing
    4. Family

Z. The Supervisor's Key to Discipline
    There are several key points about discipline which the supervisor should keep in mind:
    1. Job discipline is one of the disciplines of life and is directed by the supervisor.
    2. It is more important to correct an employee fault than to fix blame for it.
    3. Employee performance is affected by problems both on the job and off.
    4. Sudden or abrupt changes in behavior can be indications of important employee problems.
    5. Problems should be dealt with as soon as possible after they are identified.
    6. The attitude of the supervisor may have more to do with solving problems than the techniques of problem solving.
    7. Correction of employee behavior should be resorted to only after the supervisor is sure that training or counseling will not be helpful.

8. Be sure to document your disciplinary actions.
9. Make sure that you are disciplining on the basis of facts rather than personal feelings.
10. Take each disciplinary step in order, being careful not to make snap judgments, or decisions based on impatience.

AA. Five Important Processes of Management
1. Planning
2. Organizing
3. Scheduling
4. Controlling
5. Motivating

BB. When the Supervisor Fails to Plan
1. Supervisor creates impression of not knowing his job
2. May lead to excessive overtime
3. Job runs itself—supervisor lacks control
4. Deadlines and appointments missed
5. Parts of the work go undone
6. Work interrupted by emergencies
7. Sets a bad example
8. Uneven workload creates peaks and valleys
9. Too much time on minor details at expense of more important tasks

CC. Fourteen General Principles of Management
1. Division of work
2. Authority and responsibility
3. Discipline
4. Unity of command
5. Unity of direction
6. Subordination of individual interest to general interest
7. Remuneration of personnel
8. Centralization
9. Scalar chain
10. Order
11. Equity
12. Stability of tenure of personnel
13. Initiative
14. Esprit de corps

DD. Change

Bringing about change is perhaps attempted more often, and yet less well understood, than anything else the supervisor does. How do people generally react to change? (People tend to resist change that is imposed upon them by other individuals or circumstances.

Change is characteristic of every situation. It is a part of every real endeavor where the efforts of people are concerned.

1. Why do people resist change?
   People may resist change because of:
   a. Fear of the unknown
   b. Implied criticism
   c. Unpleasant experiences in the past
   d. Fear of loss of status
   e. Threat to the ego
   f. Fear of loss of economic stability

2. How can we best overcome the resistance to change?
   In initiating change, take these steps:
   a. Get ready to sell
   b. Identify sources of help
   c. Anticipate objections
   d. Sell benefits
   e. Listen in depth
   f. Follow up

II. Brief Topical Summaries

   A. Who/What is the Supervisor?
      1. The supervisor is often called the "highest level employee and the lowest level manager."
      2. A supervisor is a member of both management and the work group. He acts as a bridge between the two.
      3. Most problems in supervision are in the area of human relations, or people problems.
      4. Employees expect: Respect, opportunity to learn and to advance, and a sense of belonging, and so forth.
      5. Supervisors are responsible for directing people and organizing work. Planning is of paramount importance.
      6. A position description is a set of duties and responsibilities inherent to a given position.
      7. It is important to keep the position description up-to-date and to provide each employee with his own copy.

   B. The Sociology of Work
      1. People are alike in many ways; however, each individual is unique.
      2. The supervisor is challenged in getting to know employee differences. Acquiring skills in evaluating individuals is an asset.
      3. Maintaining meaningful working relationships in the organization is of great importance.
      4. The supervisor has an obligation to help individuals to develop to their fullest potential.
      5. Job rotation on a planned basis helps to build versatility and to maintain interest and enthusiasm in work groups.
      6. Cross training (job rotation) provides backup skills.

7. The supervisor can help reduce tension by maintaining a sense of humor, providing guidance to employees, and by making reasonable and timely decisions. Employees respond favorably to working under reasonably predictable circumstances.
8. Change is characteristic of all managerial behavior. The supervisor must adjust to changes in procedures, new methods, technological changes, and to a number of new and sometimes challenging situations.
9. To overcome the natural tendency for people to resist change, the supervisor should become more skillful in initiating change.

C. Principles and Practices of Supervision
1. Employees should be required to answer to only one superior.
2. A supervisor can effectively direct only a limited number of employees, depending upon the complexity, variety, and proximity of the jobs involved.
3. The organizational chart presents the organization in graphic form. It reflects lines of authority and responsibility as well as interrelationships of units within the organization.
4. Distribution of work can be improved through an analysis using the "Work Distribution Chart."
5. The "Work Distribution Chart" reflects the division of work within a unit in understandable form.
6. When related tasks are given to an employee, he has a better chance of increasing his skills through training.
7. The individual who is given the responsibility for tasks must also be given the appropriate authority to insure adequate results.
8. The supervisor should delegate repetitive, routine work. Preparation of recurring reports, maintaining leave and attendance records are some examples.
9. Good discipline is essential to good task performance. Discipline is reflected in the actions of employees on the job in the absence of supervision.
10. Disciplinary action may have to be taken when the positive aspects of discipline have failed. Reprimand, warning, and suspension are examples of disciplinary action.
11. If a situation calls for a reprimand, be sure it is deserved and remember it is to be done in private.

D. Dynamic Leadership
1. A style is a personal method or manner of exerting influence.
2. Authoritarian leaders often see themselves as the source of power and authority.
3. The democratic leader often perceives the group as the source of authority and power.
4. Supervisors tend to do better when using the pattern of leadership that is most natural for them.
5. Social scientists suggest that the effective supervisor use the leadership style that best fits the problem or circumstances involved.
6. All four styles—telling, selling, consulting, joining—have their place. Using one does not preclude using the other at another time.

7. The theory X point of view assumes that the average person dislikes work, will avoid it whenever possible, and must be coerced to achieve organizational objectives.
8. The theory Y point of view assumes that the average person considers work to be a natural as play, and, when the individual is committed, he requires little supervision or direction to accomplish desired objectives.
9. The leader's basic assumptions concerning human behavior and human nature affect his actions, decisions, and other managerial practices.
10. Dissatisfaction among employees is often present, but difficult to isolate. The supervisor should seek to weaken dissatisfaction by keeping promises, being sincere and considerate, keeping employees informed, and so forth.
11. Constructive suggestions should be encouraged during the natural progress of the work.

E. Processes for Solving Problems
1. People find their daily tasks more meaningful and satisfying when they can improve them.
2. The causes of problems, or the key factors, are often hidden in the background. Ability to solve problems often involves the ability to isolate them from their backgrounds. There is some substance to the cliché that some persons "can't see the forest for the trees."
3. New procedures are often developed from old ones. Problems should be broken down into manageable parts. New ideas can be adapted from old one.
4. People think differently in problem-solving situations. Using a logical, patterned approach is often useful. One approach found to be useful includes these steps:
   a. Define the problem
   b. Establish objectives
   c. Get the facts
   d. Weigh and decide
   e. Take action
   f. Evaluate action

F. Training for Results
1. Participants respond best when they feel training is important to them.
2. The supervisor has responsibility for the training and development of those who report to him.
3. When training is delegated to others, great care must be exercised to insure the trainer has knowledge, aptitude, and interest for his work as a trainer.
4. Training (learning) of some type goes on continually. The most successful supervisor makes certain the learning contributes in a productive manner to operational goals.
5. New employees are particularly susceptible to training. Older employees facing new job situations require specific training, as well as having need for development and growth opportunities.
6. Training needs require continuous monitoring.
7. The training officer of an agency is a professional with a responsibility to assist supervisors in solving training problems.

8. Many of the self-development steps important to the supervisor's own growth are equally important to the development of peers and subordinates. Knowledge of these is important when the supervisor consults with others on development and growth opportunities.

G. Health, Safety, and Accident Prevention
1. Management-minded supervisors take appropriate measures to assist employees in maintaining health and in assuring safe practices in the work environment.
2. Effective safety training and practices help to avoid injury and accidents.
3. Safety should be a management goal. All infractions of safety which are observed should be corrected without exception.
4. Employees' safety attitude, training and instruction, provision of safe tools and equipment, supervision, and leadership are considered highly important factors which contribute to safety and which can be influenced directly by supervisors.
5. When accidents do occur, they should be investigated promptly for very important reasons, including the fact that information which is gained can be used to prevent accidents in the future.

H. Equal Employment Opportunity
1. The supervisor should endeavor to treat all employees fairly, without regard to religion, race, sex, or national origin.
2. Groups tend to reflect the attitude of the leader. Prejudice can be detected even in very subtle form. Supervisors must strive to create a feeling of mutual respect and confidence in every employee.
3. Complete utilization of all human resources is a national goal. Equitable consideration should be accorded women in the work force, minority-group members, the physically and mentally handicapped, and the older employee. The important question is: "Who can do the job?"
4. Training opportunities, recognition for performance, overtime assignments, promotional opportunities, and all other personnel actions are to be handled on an equitable basis.

I. Improving Communications
1. Communications is achieving understanding between the sender and the receiver of a message. It also means sharing information—the creation of understanding.
2. Communication is basic to all human activity. Words are means of conveying meanings; however, real meanings are in people.
3. There are very practical differences in the effectiveness of one-way, impersonal, and two-way communications. Words spoken face-to-face are better understood. Telephone conversations are effective, but lack the rapport of person-to-person exchanges. The whole person communicates.
4. Cooperation and communication in an organization go hand in hand. When there is a mutual respect between people, spelling out rules and procedures for communicating is unnecessary.
5. There are several barriers to effective communications. These include failure to listen with respect and understanding, lack of skill in feedback, and misinterpreting the meanings of words used by the speaker. It is also common

practice to listen to what we want to hear, and tune out things we do not want to hear.
6. Communication is management's chief problem. The supervisor should accept the challenge to communicate more effectively and to improve interagency and intra-agency communications.
7. The supervisor may often plan for and conduct meetings. The planning phase is critical and may determine the success or the failure of a meeting.
8. Speaking before groups usually requires extra effort. Stage fright may never disappear completely, but it can be controlled.

J. Self-Development
1. Every employee is responsible for his own self-development.
2. Toastmaster and toastmistress clubs offer opportunities to improve skills in oral communications.
3. Planning for one's own self-development is of vital importance. Supervisors know their own strengths and limitations better than anyone else.
4. Many opportunities are open to aid the supervisor in his developmental efforts, including job assignments; training opportunities, both governmental and non-governmental—to include universities and professional conferences and seminars.
5. Programmed instruction offers a means of studying at one's own rate.
6. Where difficulties may arise from a supervisor's being away from his work for training, he may participate in televised home study or correspondence courses to meet his self-development needs.

K. Teaching and Training
1. The Teaching Process
Teaching is encouraging and guiding the learning activities of students toward established goals. In most cases this process consists of five steps: preparation, presentation, summarization, evaluation, and application.

   a. Preparation
   Preparation is two-fold in nature; that of the supervisor and the employee. Preparation by the supervisor is absolutely essential to success. He must know what, when, where, how, and whom he will teach. Some of the factors that should be considered are:
   1) The objectives
   2) The materials needed
   3) The methods to be used
   4) Employee participation
   5) Employee interest
   6) Training aids
   7) Evaluation
   8) Summarization

   Employee preparation consists in preparing the employee to receive the material. Probably the most important single factor in the preparation of the employee is arousing and maintaining his interest. He must know the objectives of the training, why he is there, how the material can be used, and its importance to him.

b. Presentation
In presentation, have a carefully designed plan and follow it. The plan should be accurate and complete, yet flexible enough to meet situations as they arise. The method of presentation will be determined by the particular situation and objectives.

c. Summary
A summary should be made at the end of every training unit and program. In addition, there may be internal summaries depending on the nature of the material being taught. The important thing is that the trainee must always be able to understand how each part of the new material relates to the whole.

d. Application
The supervisor must arrange work so the employee will be given a chance to apply new knowledge or skills while the material is still clear in his mind and interest is high. The trainee does not really know whether he has learned the material until he has been given a chance to apply it. If the material is not applied, it loses most of its value.

e. Evaluation
The purpose of all training is to promote learning. To determine whether the training has been a success or failure, the supervisor must evaluate this learning.
In the broadest sense, evaluation includes all the devices, methods, skills, and techniques used by the supervisor to keep himself and the employees informed as to their progress toward the objectives they are pursuing. The extent to which the employee has mastered the knowledge, skills, and abilities, or changed his attitudes, as determined by the program objectives, is the extent to which instruction has succeeded or failed.
Evaluation should not be confined to the end of the lesson, day, or program but should be used continuously. We shall note later the way this relates to the rest of the teaching process.

2. Teaching Methods
A teaching method is a pattern of identifiable student and instructor activity used in presenting training material.
All supervisors are faced with the problem of deciding which method should be used at a given time.

a. Lecture
The lecture is direct oral presentation of material by the supervisor. The present trend is to place less emphasis on the trainer's activity and more on that of the trainee.

b. Discussion
Teaching by discussion or conference involves using questions and other techniques to arouse interest and focus attention upon certain areas, and by doing so creating a learning situation. This can be one of the most

valuable methods because it gives the employees an opportunity to express their ideas and pool their knowledge.

    c. Demonstration
The demonstration is used to teach how something works or how to do something. It can be used to show a principle or what the results of a series of actions will be. A well-staged demonstration is particularly effective because it shows proper methods of performance in a realistic manner.

    d. Performance
Performance is one of the most fundamental of all learning techniques or teaching methods. The trainee may be able to tell how a specific operation should be performed but he cannot be sure he knows how to perform the operation until he has done so.
As with all methods, there are certain advantages and disadvantages to each method.

    e. Which Method to Use
Moreover, there are other methods and techniques of teaching. It is difficult to use any method without other methods entering into it. In any learning situation, a combination of methods is usually more effective than any one method alone.

Finally, evaluation must be integrated into the other aspects of the teaching-learning process.

It must be used in the motivation of the trainees; it must be used to assist in developing understanding during the training; and it must be related to employee application of the results of training.

This is distinctly the role of the supervisor.

190